Encyclopedia

of

AIRLINE

COLOUR

SCHEMES

By IAN MACKINTOSH

VOLUME I

NORTH AMERICA   Part I

ISBN   0 905117 51 4
ISSN   0142 − 629X

Published by: AIRLINE PUBLICATIONS & SALES LTD.
Noble Corner
Great West Road
Hounslow
Middlesex TW5 0PA.
Telephone: 01-572 0225

Printed by: RUSKIN PRESS LTD.,
138/146 Cambridge Heath Road,
London E1 5QJ.
Telephone: 01-790 3157

Colour Separation by: COTTRELL & McGUIRE REPRODUCTIONS LTD.
Stanway Street,
London N.1.
Telephone: 01-729 2140

AUTHOR'S FOREWORD

THERE is a saying in the industry that an airline's livery is chosen by the chairman's wife, and that thus the livery changes when a new chairman arrives. But that is fair neither to bachelor-chairmen, nor to those top livery designers — such as Landor Associates and Saul Bass — who are a creative force and a vital factor in the presentation of an airline's image. In these days of cut-price fares and fierce competition over fixed routes, it is essential to an airline's survival that it takes precedence in the public memory over its rivals; and liveries can make airlines unforgettable, and can make aircraft look clean, smart, efficient and inviting.

Catalina Airlines' Goose amphibians may be around forty years old; but the livery keeps them young at heart. Alaska Airlines' Eskimo has a smiling face; and smiling faces win friends. McCully Aviation's little Beavers prove that one does not need a gleaming jet or a complicated scheme to make an aeroplane look bright and businesslike.

It is a fascinating — and a colourful — subject; and I hope that you, the reader, will stay with us through the six or so companion volumes yet to come. Volume II will illustrate 152 European airlines; and later volumes will cover Central and South America, Africa, the Middle East and Asia, the Far East and Australasia, and more Canadian and US airlines. As with this volume, later books will carry, where appropriate, the logo or motif of each featured airline, in colour.

Finally, my thanks to the many airlines who answered my letters and telephone calls; to Russell Brown for help in numerous ways; and to John Kimberley, who took almost one-third of the photographs in this volume, and without whose enthusiasm (and cameras) I could not have completed the work in the given timescale.

London, England
November 1978.

I.M.

1. ACADEMY AIRLINES

Academy Airlines, based at Griffin-Spalding County Airport, Griffin, Georgia, operates both passenger and cargo charters and undertakes also shorter commissions as a form of air-taxi. The airline holds authority to work throughout the United States, and to Canada, the Bahamas and the West Indies; and is under contract to the US Post Office as a carrier of the US Mail.

The company operates currently with three DC-3 aircraft, registered N130D, N133D and N143D.

Although extremely simple, the livery looks very effective on the DC-3. The fuselage is white overall, with narrow cheatlines in two values of blue; the airline titling, in the lighter blue, is in an attractive script form; and the company logo, on the tail-fin, is a stylised double   "A". Note also the black anti-dazzle panel on the nose, and the neatly-curtained passenger windows!

2. AEROAMERICA

Aeroamerica began operations in January 1974, having its origins in the now-defunct travel club Air Club International. Its headquarters are at Seattle in Washington state; and it operates a European division from Tegel Airport, Berlin, with a regional office in Cairo, Egypt.

Intra-state services are flown between Seattle and Spokane; while in Europe, inclusive-tours reach points as distant from Berlin as Eire, Turkey and the Canary Islands. Cargo-charter work is also undertaken, mainly in Africa and the Middle East. The current fleet consists of 8 B.720s, 3 B.707s and an Aero Commander.

Aeroamerica's aircraft boast a colourful but baffling variety of liveries. The "globe" tail logo is consistent in size and shape, but may change colour to match one of the colours in the double (or sometimes triple) cheatline, and the fuselage roof is usually in white. Not even this can be taken as a rule of thumb, however, because one aircraft (N733T) has a "double thickness" cheatline in white, with a red roof and mustard underside. Equally, the airline titling can be in white, blue or pink.

(Insignia — Plate 1)

3.   **AEROBEC**

Aerobec, with its headquarters at Ste-Foy, Quebec, was formed on 13 April 1973; and today conducts charter business across Canada (but primarily in Quebec, Ontario, Manitoba and the Maritime Provinces) and in the eastern USA. Additionally, in 1978, the airline acquired a Class 3 licence to fly non-scheduled services linking Quebec City and Montreal with Thetford-Mines and Trois-Rivières. Aerobec operates also the biggest flying school in Quebec province, and undertakes aircraft repairs, overhaul, sales and consultant services.

The airline uses a mixed fleet of some 17 aircraft, including a PA-31 Navajo Chieftain, a PA-31T Cheyenne, a PA-34 Seneca, 8 PA-28 Cherokees, 3 Aerostar 600s, a Cessna 310 and 2 Cessna 172s.

The Aerobec fleet operates in a variety of liveries — which differ even between aircraft of the same type — but perhaps the most attractive is that illustrated on Aerostar C-GQTP. Moreover, the block-lettered airline titling is standard; as is the carrying of the company logo — a red circle with blue and red stripes leading from it — and generally, the logo is worn immediately adjacent to the titling. Note, however, that the "chevron" motif on the tail-fin is not an airline symbol, but is carried by all Aerostar aircraft.

(Insignia — Plate 1)

4.   **AERO-DYNE AIRLINES**

Aero-Dyne Airlines, a division of the Aero-Dyne Corporation based at Renton, Washington, was incorporated in 1965; and offers passenger charter and air taxi services, cargo charter and contract, warm fog dispersal (Aero-Dyne is the largest and oldest continuous operator in the field of warm fog dispersal at major airline terminals), aerial application of chemicals, seed, beneficial insects and fertilizer, and aircraft leasing. A comprehensive flight school and a major maintenance base are also operated by the airline.

Aero-Dyne's fleet numbers 19 aircraft: 9 DC-3s, a CV.440, a CV.240 and 8 light aircraft which include a Cessna 150 and a Beech 95 Baron.

The livery is a cleverly-designed combination of white, red and brown, and sits particularly well on the DC-3. The double-cheatline in red and brown is so arranged that not only does it decorate the tail-fin in a large and stylised "A"; but manages also to encompass the "arrow" symbol for'ard. Thus, the entire airline logo (see colour plate thereof) is set along the length of the aircraft. Airline titling is in large, brown block letters, on the white fuselage roof.

(Insignia — Plate 4)

1. Academy's Douglas DC-3, N143D at Griffin, Georgia, on 2 August 1976 .

(Photograph by IAS, P. Van Damme)

2. Aeroamerica's Boeing 720-027, N734T in July 1976.   (Photograph from author's private collection)

3. Aerobec's Smith Aerostar 600 C-GQTP at Toronto on 11 February 1978.
(Photograph by Russell Brown)

4. Aero-Dyne's Douglas DC-3, N44587 in August 1978.　　(Photograph by John Kimberley)

5.   AIR CALIFORNIA

Air California began operations in January 1967 with two ex-American Electras, and is today a wholly-owned subsidiary of Westgate-California. Its headquarters are at Newport Beach, and the airline offers high-frequency intra-state passenger services between San Diego, Orange County-Disneyland, Palm Springs, Ontario, San Jose, San Francisco, Oakland, Sacramento and Lake Tahoe.

The Air California fleet consists of 9 B.737s and 3 L.188C Electras, these last being used primarily on services to Lake Tahoe.

Until April 1978, Air California's livery was predominantly white and yellow; but in that month, the entire fleet was repainted in a revised scheme, developed by the airline's advertising agency, Phillips Ramsey of San Diego. The scheme retains the lines and styling of the old livery; but makes the yellow and orange cheatlines much broader (for greater in-flight visibility), has airline titling in brown (was red), and the "sunburst" logo on the tail — and contoured around the nose — is also now in brown (was yellow on a white surround). Aircraft interiors have been redesigned, too, in complementary colours.

(Insignia — Plate 3)

6.   AIR CANADA

Air Canada was formed on 10 April 1937 as Trans-Canada Air Lines, and took its current name in 1964. Its headquarters are in Montreal; and, as the State airline, it operates a very large network of scheduled passenger and cargo services within Canada, and has international routes to the USA, the West Indies and European destinations which include Copenhagen, Shannon, Prestwick, London, Paris, Frankfurt and Zurich.

A mixed all-jet fleet of over 110 aircraft is operated, with B.747s, B.727s, L.1011s, DC-8s and DC-9s.

Until early 1977, Air Canada had retained the same livery since the change of name in 1964. In 1977, however, a revised livery appeared, which altered the shade of the cheatline and tail-fin to a warmer, more "orange" red, dispensed with the black anti-dazzle nose panel, took the cheatline "straight through" and under the tail (it was cut off previously just for'ard of the tail-unit), put airline titling into the same orange-red instead of black, and lost the small company logo which was worn formerly adjacent to the titling.

This new livery, although simpler than its predecessor, is held generally to be smarter; and, of course, the logo continues to dominate the tail-fin, still as a white maple-leaf within a white circle, broken at the "stem" of the leaf.

(Insignia — Plate 3)

7. AIR CORTEZ

Air Cortez of Ontario, California, was certificated on 5 April 1977, and operates commuter services from Ontario to Loreto, Mexicali, Mulege and San Felipe, all in the Baja California peninsula of Mexico. Additionally, the airline undertakes charter work throughout the western USA and into the Baja area.

The current fleet numbers 6 aircraft: 2 Beech 18s, a Cessna 411, a Cessna 412 and 2 Cessna 182s. The airline plans to acquire also 2 CV.240/440s in the near future.

Beech 18 N139V was the first aircraft to be painted up in the current livery (in mid-1978); and the scheme consists of an all-white fuselage, with twin cheatlines in red and gold, these colours being repeated also on the engines. Airline titling is in an attractive black lettering; and the company logo, worn on the outboard side of the tail-fins is in red, orange, gold and yellow.

8. AIR-DALE

Air-Dale of Sault Ste. Marie in Ontario, began operations in 1946 as Airdale Flying Service, and took its current name ten years later. The airline serves a number of communities within Ontario, undertaking a variety of charter services to link specific terminals, and offers also an aircraft maintenance facility.

Air-Dale has currently a mixed fleet of some 13 aircraft, which include two DC-3s (registered C-FWGO and C-GRMH), a Twin Otter, an Otter and two Beavers.

The livery, as illustrated on the DC-3, is extremely simple, consisting of a white upper and light-grey lower fuselage, divided by an orangey-red cheatline which matches the colour of the tail-fin.

Note that the black airline titling includes the word "Ltd" — a practice more prevelant, perhaps, among Canadian airlines that those of any other country.

(Insignia — Plate 4)

5. Air California's Boeing 737-293, N462GB at San Francisco on 12 May 1978.

(Photograph by the author)

6. Air Canada's McDonnell Douglas DC-9-32 C-FTLR at Toronto on 30 July 1978.

(Photograph by Russell Brown)

7. Air Cortez's Beech 18, N139V at Ontario in August 1978. (Photograph by John Wegg)

8. Air-Dale's Douglas DC-3, C-FWGO in September 1977. (Photograph from APS files)

9. AIR FLORIDA

Air Florida of Miami was formed in September 1971 and began operations in September 1972 as an intra-state (Florida) carrier. The airline now links Miami International Airport with Gainesville, Jacksonville, Orlando, Tallahassee and Tampa.

Air Florida's current fleet consists of 5 DC-9-15s; but until early 1977, the airline used Electras, in an orange and red livery. It was then that Air Florida leased a B.727 (N40AF) from International Air Leases, and this B.727 brought with it an entirely new scheme; with an orange roof; a blue, white-edged cheatline; red airline titling beneath the cheatline for'ard, and a new and stylised "AF" in white on the tail-fin.

From August 1977, however, the Electras and the B.727 were phased out and sold, and replaced by the DC-9s; and another new livery, evolving from the B.727 livery, appeared: the airline titling, now in white, has moved above the cheatline; and the white band beneath the blue cheat is much broader, and in effect makes for a double-cheatline. But note the retention of the white trim above the blue.

(Insignia — Plate 3)

10. AIR GASPÉ

Air Gaspé of Havre de Gaspé, Quebec, was formed in March 1952 as Trans-Gaspian Airlines, to fly charter operations in the Gaspé Peninsula; and today offers scheduled passenger and cargo services to link Gaspé with House Harbour, Port Menier, Mont Joli, Havre St. Pierre, Bonaventure, Sept-Iles, Quebec City and the Magdalen Islands (all in Quebec) and Charlo in New Brunswick. The airline undertakes also charters throughout Canada, and aerial survey and photography.

The current fleet numbers 4 aircraft: an HS.748, 2 PA-31 Navajos and a Beech 99.

The livery, which has been unchanged for many years and is largely common to the HS.748 and the smaller aircraft, consists of a wide blue, black-trimmed cheatline with a blue and black stylised "dart" shape on the fin; but note that while the smaller types have an all-white fuselage, the HS.748 is bare-metal beneath the lower trimline. The airline titling is always in red, and in script form; but again, the HS.748 has slightly different styling to the smaller types, and does not carry the word "Inc" thereafter. Note too, the blue wing-tips on the Navajos.

(Insignia — Plate 4)

11. AIR ILLINOIS

Air Illinois of Carbondale, Illinois, was formed in 1970 to operate third-level scheduled services, within its home state, but extended thereafter to serve additionally such points as Cape Girardeau and St. Louis in Missouri, Memphis in Tennessee, and Jonesboro in Arkansas. Then, in December 1977, the airline took over South Central Air Transport (SCAT), thereby extending further to Alabama, Florida and Louisiana.

Air Illinois's current fleet consists of 3 Twin Otters, 4 Jetstreams (with 2 more on order) and 1 HS.748. This HS.748 is used to operate into Meigs Field, Chicago's "downtown" airport, which — while much more convenient to commuters than O'Hare International — is situated on the waterfront, with a very short runway length, and thus is denied normally to "large" aircraft. The HS.748's ability to cope safely with this restriction has been, therefore, a most valuable bonus to the airline's development.

The airline's livery looks particularly effective on the HS.748, with its simple styling complementing the functional lines of the aircraft. Note that the small logos, on the tail-fin and at the for'ard end of the blue and green cheatlines, have the "aircraft" therein always pointing forward.

(Insignia — Plate 2)

12. AIRLIFT INTERNATIONAL

Airlift International was formed in May 1945 as the Riddle Aviation Company, became Riddle Airlines in 1952, and took its current corporate identity in 1964. The fleet and assets of Slick Airways were acquired in 1968. Based at Miami International Airport, Airlift is certificated as a scheduled all-cargo carrier with routes throughout the United States and to Puerto Rico and the US Virgin Islands; but undertakes additionally both passenger and cargo charters, and military contract work, worldwide.

Airlift leases out its own aircraft, and takes leases on others, but operates officially with 3 DC-8-63CFs, 2 DC-8-50Fs, 3 DC-8-30Fs and a B.727-100C.

Because of leasing arrangements, the airline operates aircraft in a variety of liveries; but its own corporate livery — as illustrated — is readily identifiable, with the narrow twin-cheatlines, the company logo on both tail-fin and nose, and airline titling in bold, block letters on the upper fuselage.

(Insignia — Plate 4)

9. Air Florida's DC-9-15F N75AF in April 1978.   (Photograph by IAPS, J. Plaisier)

10. Air Gaspé's Piper PA-31 Navajo CF-YFJ in August 1970.   (Photograph from APS files)

11. Air Illinois' Hawker Siddeley HS.748-2A N748LL in November, 1974.
(Photograph from author's private collection)

12. Airlift's McDonnell Douglas DC-8-63CF N6163A in April 1978.
(Photograph by IAPS, J. Plaisier)

13. AIR MIDWEST

Air Midwest of Wichita, Kansas, was certificated in November 1976 as a regional
feeder air carrier; and serves Wichita, Dodge City, Garden City, Goodland, Great
Bend, Hays, Hutchinson and Parsons (all in Kansas), Denver and Lamar in Colorado,
and Kansas City in Missouri.

The airline's fleet consists of 5 Metroliner IIs, registered in sequence from N223AM
to N227AM.

At first sight, Air Midwest's livery gives an impression of smart simplicity; but is, in
fact, cleverly designed. Note that the triple cheatline — in light brown, yellow and
red — runs for almost its entire length as a solid composition, but separates in the
sweep up to the tail, to leave white "gaps" between the colours; cheatline colours
are repeated on the engine nacelles, which are metal-finish on top and white beneath;
the "tail sweep" is repeated, too, in the airline logo forward of the passenger windows.

Note also that airline titling is small-lettered, while aircraft registrations are bold.
(Insignia — Plate 2)

14. AIR NEW ENGLAND

Air New England of East Boston, Massachusetts, was formed in October 1970 as a
scheduled commuter airline, and was subsequently certificated as a regional air
carrier on 24 January 1975. This certification, and CAB approval for Air New
England to take up routes relinquished in the local area by Delta, put the airline on
the map — both literally and figuratively. Today, the airline serves Boston, Hyannis,
Nantucket, Martha's Vineyard and New Bedford in Massachusetts; Keene and
Lebanon in New Hampshire; Portland, Lewiston, Augusta and Waterville in Maine;
Burlington and Montpelier in Vermont; and New York (La Guardia).

Air New England's current fleet consists of 6 FH-227s and 10 Twin Otters.

Highlight of the livery is the double-cheatline, in purple and blue, which fans out
and up over the tail to enclose two other stripes in orange and green. Note also the
unusual airline titling; and the fact that wing and tailplane surfaces are all-white,
except for leading-edge de-icer boots.
(Insignia — Plate 4)

15. AIR SUNSHINE

Air Sunshine of Key West, Florida, is the schedule-services division of AAT airlines which, as American Air Taxi Inc, was formed in 1951. The title of Air Sunshine was adopted in 1972. The airline, which bills itself as "The Florida Keys Own Airline", flies scheduled passenger services solely within the state of Florida, serving Key West, Miami, Marathon, Kissimmee/Orlando and Tampa. Charters are also undertaken.

Until late 1977, Air Sunshine operated 4 DC-3s only; but has added since 2 CV.440s, giving now a total fleet of 6 aircraft.

As befits the airline's name, the livery is bright; with double cheatlines in orange and yellow, sweeping up to the tail. Note, too, the black trim beneath the lower cheatline, the "sun" just forward of the airline titling, and the fact that — on the DC-3s — the airline titling is in black, slightly-stylised letters edged in yellow; while the CV.440s have plain black, block letters.

(Insignia — Plate 2)

16. AIR WEST

Air West, or Airwest Airlines Ltd, of Vancouver, British Columbia, began scheduled services in 1964, and uses float-equipped aircraft for "downtown" access to cities and for services to remoter regions. Such a "downtown" operation is that used between Vancouver and Victoria, Nanaimo and Duncan (Quamichan Lake); while more conventional services link Vancouver International Airport with airports at Nanaimo and Texada Island. Charter work is also undertaken; and an international route is operated between Victoria Harbour and Seattle (Lake Union) in Washington state, USA.

Air West's fleet comprises some 24 aircraft, including 7 Twin Otters, 4 Beavers, 3 Turbo Beavers, 2 Turbo Goose amphibians, an Otter and an Islander.

Although some of Air West's very small aircraft and one of the two Goose amphibians are in non-standard livery, all other aircraft share the illustrated scheme of an all-white fuselage, twin cheatlines in red and orange, and the company logo, in black, just for'ard of the fuselage waist. On the Twin Otters, the cheatlines go around the nose, and are reflected also up the trailing-edge of the tail-fin.

(Insignia — Plate 3)

13. Air Midwest's Swearingen SA226TC Metroliner II N226AM on 12 June 1978.
(Photograph by J.H. Williamson)

14. Air New England's Fairchild-Hiller FH-227C N378NE in January 1975.
(Photograph by R.R. Leader)

15. Air Sunshine's Convair CV.440 N477KW in April 1978.   (Photograph by IAPS, J. Plaisier)

16. Air West's de Havilland Canada DHC-3 Otter C-FXRI on floats in August 1978.
(Photograph by John Kimberley)

17. AIR WISCONSIN

Air Wisconsin is one of the largest commuter airlines in the United States, has operated scheduled services since August 1965, and now serves communities in the states of Wisconsin, Illinois, Indiana, Michigan, Minnesota and Nebraska, from its base at Outagamie Airport, Appleton, Wisconsin. Air freight and mail are carried, in addition to the passengers, across the route-network.

Air Wisconsin's fleet consists of 12 Metroliners, making the airline one of the principal users of the type in the world; and 2 Dash 7s are on order.

The livery, designed by Gordon Fischer Advertising, is simple but striking; with airline titles and the lower cheatline in green, and the upper cheatline in orange. Note, however, that in the logo on the tail-fin, the leading letter is always in orange, and the after letter is always green. Thus, on the starboard side of the tail, the "W" is in orange, and the "A" in green; while on the port side, the reverse applies.

(Insignia — Plate 1)

18. ALASKA AIRLINES

Alaska Airlines has its headquarters at Seattle in Washington state, began life in 1930 as Star Air Service, operating from Anchorage, Alaska, and adopted its present title in 1943. In 1968, it absorbed Cordova Airlines and Alaska Coastal Airlines; and to-day, offers extensive services in the state of Alaska, and to Seattle, with a fleet of 10 B.727-100s and 2 B.727-200s.

The airline has been always a leader in original and colourful livery design, having gone from the famous "Golden Nugget jet" promotional scheme to the delightful "Alaskana Graphics" liveries, which illustrated Alaskan subjects on the tail-fins of the aircraft: Gold Rush Alaska (a prospector, in red); Indian Alaska (an Indian carving, in green); Russian Alaska ("onion-domed" buildings, in purple); and Eskimo Alaska (an Eskimo head, in blue). The last of these was the most popular; and since 1977, all aircraft have gone into the Eskimo Head scheme, with some revisions thereto: the Eskimo smiles now (where once he frowned!), large airline titling on the tail-engine has been omitted, and cheatlines (now in blue and green) are modified to run above and below the passenger windows.

(Insignia — Plate 1)

19. ALASKA INTERNATIONAL AIR

Alaska International Air of Fairbanks, Alaska, was formed in 1946 as Interior Airways, to operate various Alaskan charter services with light aircraft, took its current name in September 1972 and is now a cargo charter airline within a group of companies headed by Alaska International Industries Inc. The airline operates scheduled cargo flights within Alaska, and cargo charters worldwide.

Alaska International Air's current fleet consists of 5 L.100-30 Hercules, having the ability, of course, to land on small remote airstrips. In addition, when on contract work, the airline can provide its own runway-lighting system, radio beacons etc, to create an "instant airport" for the Hercules.

The livery consists of a blue cheatline, doubled-up for'ard to house the airline titling, with a blue tail and stylised company motif thereon, in white and gold. Note also the thin gold trimline between the cheatlines; and that the aircraft is basically in a natural metal finish.

(Insignia — Plate 3)

20. ALLEGHENY AIRLINES

Allegheny Airlines of Washington, DC. was established in 1937 as All-American Airways to pioneer "pick-up" mail services. More conventional scheduled services began in 1949, and the airline took its current name in 1953. Mergers with Lake Central Airlines (1968) and Mohawk Airlines (1972) gave Allegheny access to more than 100 city-terminals; and today Allegheny covers practically every major city in the northeastern USA, with international routes to Montreal and Toronto in Canada. The airline established the Allegheny Commuter system (see entry for Ransome Airlines) to expand operations to smaller terminals along the route-network, in the late 1960s.

Allegheny's current fleet numbers some 90 aircraft; an all-jet mix of BAC-111s, DC-9s and 727-100s.

The livery, developed by Landor Associates of San Francisco and first seen on DC-9 N979VJ on 12 May 1975, features a single horizontal stripe running the length of the fuselage; beginning in a light shade of red and blending progressively into three darker shades before sweeping up and fanning out in all four shades on the tail-fin.

The Allegheny Commuter livery, introduced in 1977, is illustrated under Ransome Airlines.

(Insignia — Plate 4)

17. Air Wisconsin's Swearingen SA226TC Metroliner N424S at Appleton.
(Photograph by IAS, P. Van Damme)

18. Alaska's Boeing 727-21 N316AS at Seattle in November 1977. (Photograph by Drew Ewbank)

19. Alaska International Air's Lockheed L.100-30 Hercules N104AK in October 1976.

(Photograph by APN)

20. Allegheny's McDonnell Douglas DC-9-31 N993VJ in August 1978.

(Photograph from author's private collection)

21. ALOHA AIRLINES

Aloha Airlines of Honolulu was formed in June 1946 as Trans-Pacific Airlines, and changed its name to Aloha in November 1958. The airline operates over a 356-mile network in the state of Hawaii, serving 6 points on the 5 islands of Oahu, Kauai, Molokai, Maui and Hawaii.

In its time, the airline has used DC-3s, F-27s, Viscounts and BAC-111s; but has standardised now on a fleet of 2 B.737-100s and 6 B.737-200s.

The livery is typically Hawaiian and was indeed designed by the airline's advertising agency — Fawcett, McDermott, Cavanagh. The flower design is in the company's colours of red, orange and yellow; and of course, the name Aloha represents not only the name of the airline, but the traditional Hawaiian greeting of welcome. Note that the current livery is slightly different to the original floral livery introduced in 1969 on the first Aloha B.737. The cheatline is now underlined with a thin gold trim, and is revised to broaden towards the after fuselage and sweep up to meet the livery on the fin. Also, the new form of airline titling, with its stylised "A", replaces the old "Aloha Airlines" title and the Bird of Paradise motif.

(Insignia — Plate 2)

22. ALTAIR AIRLINES

Altair Airlines of Philadelphia was formed in October 1967 and provides comprehensive commuter services over an extensive route-network which connects Philadelphia with Washington, DC; Richmond in Virginia; Baltimore in Maryland; Wilmington in Delaware; Wilkes-Barre/Scranton, Allentown/Bethlehem/Easton and Harrisburg/York in Pennsylvania; and White Plains, Islip and New York City (JFK) in New York.

The airline operates a fleet of 6 Nord 262As and 6 Beech 99s.

Highlight of the livery is the "blue eagle" motif worn on the tail-fin. Note, however, that while both Nord 262s and Beech 99s have a white fuselage overall, there are differences in the schemes used by each type; the Nord 262 has a wide red cheatline, trimmed in blue, which runs aft in a zig-zag to go up the for'ard part of the tail-fin, while the Beech 99 has a thin, "straight-through" cheatline which is repeated in a parallel line across the root of the tail-fin; the Nord 262 has airline titling in blue and red (as illustrated) beneath the cheatline, while the Beech 99 has smaller, all-blue titles on the tail-fin; the Nord 262 has its registration in black beneath the cheatline aft, while the Beech 99's registration is in blue, and set between the two "cheatlines" on the upper after fuselage; and the Nord 262 has a distinctive, black anti-dazzle panel on the nose.

(Insignia — Plate 3)

23. AMERICAN AIRLINES

American Airlines of New York can trace its history back to 1926 and to a number of small pioneer companies which were amalgamated by the formation in 1930 of American Airways. This, in turn, became American Airlines on 13 May 1934. Today, the airline operates an extensive passenger and cargo network across the continental United States, and to Hawaii; with international routes to Canada, Mexico and the Caribbean.

American's fleet consists of more than 270 aircraft, with B.747s, DC-10-10s, B.707s and B.727s.

The current livery was introduced in April 1969, replacing the longstanding "orange lightning-stripe" scheme. The eagle became "slimmer and trimmer", in a new stylised form, to perch between the red and blue AA on the tail; while airline titles went to a bright red, outlined in white, and the triple blue, white and red cheatline added a patriotic touch. Note, also, that freighter aircraft carry the title "American Freighter"; with the word "Freighter" in the same lettering style as the main title, but in blue with the white outlining. American B.747s are dubbed "Astroliners", while the DC-10s are called "LuxuryLiners".

(Insignia — Plate 1)

24. ANTILLES AIR BOATS

Antilles Air Boats of St. Croix, US Virgin Islands, was formed in February 1964 by the late Captain Charles Blair, then a senior Pan Am pilot, using one Grumman Goose amphibian on trips between St. Croix and St. Thomas (also in the US Virgin Islands). Today, Antilles Air Boats calls itself "the world's largest seaplane airline", operating well over a hundred daily flights in the US Virgin Islands, and to the British Virgin Islands, Puerto Rico and the Dutch and French Antilles.

Antilles Air Boats' current fleet consists of some 22 aircraft; mainly Grumman Goose amphibians, but including 2 Short Sandringham flying-boats — "Excalibur VIII" (N158J) and "Southern Cross" (VP-LVE). In recent years, one of these Sandringhams has spent the summer on the eastern side of the Atlantic, operating pleasure-flights in Ireland (with Aer Arann) and on the English south coast.

The livery differs slightly for different types of aircraft: the Sandringham has a double-cheatline in red and black, and a red tail; while the Goose has a single red cheatline (with a thin red trim) which turns up into an all-white tail. The company's bird motif is in a white circle on the Sandringham's red tail; and in a red circle against the Goose's white tail, appearing additionally on the Goose in the cheatline for'ard.

(Insignia — Plate 3)

21. Aloha's Boeing 737-284 N70721 "King Lunalilo" in April 1978.　　(Photograph from APS files)

22. Altair's Nord Aviation N.262A N7885A at New York (JFK) in September 1977.
(Photograph from author's private collection)

23. American's McDonnell Douglas DC-10-10 N128AA at San Francisco on 25 May 1978.
(Photograph by the author)

24. Antilles Air Boats' Short Sandringham VP-LVE at Calshot during its "summer tour" in September 1977 (note the small Aer Arann titles).　(Photograph from author's private collection)

25. ARGOSY AIR LINES

Formed in the mid-seventies, Argosy Air Lines is a relatively new charter carrier, operating both passenger and cargo services throughout the United States and to Central and South America and the Caribbean, from its base at Fort Lauderdale International Airport, Florida.

The current fleet consists of three DC-3s and one Beech D18S. The Beech 18 and one DC-3 (N407D) have red airline titles, a double-cheatline in two tones of blue and a tail-fin motif which is a forward-pointing double-V shape in the same two tones. The second DC-3 (N14931) is in a similar livery but without the tail-fin motif; and the third DC-3 (N18196) is in a quite different livery, with a broad red, black-trimmed cheatline which sweeps up to arc across the tail-fin, although the red airline titling is the same as that on its sister aircraft. All four aircraft have all-white fuselages, and black-tipped noses.

26. ASPEN AIRWAYS

Aspen Airways of Denver, Colorado, was established in 1962 as an air-taxi operator and in January 1966, received CAB approval to operate larger aircraft; being then granted its "certificate of public convenience and necessity" on 9 March 1967. Today, Aspen remains the smallest certificated air carrier in the USA, having only one year-round scheduled route: that between Denver and Aspen (a celebrated Colorado ski-resort) some 113 miles away. The route is know accordingly as the "the world's fastest ski-lift". In addition Aspen holds authority for charter work within the USA, and to Canada and Mexico.

The current fleet consists of 7 CV.580s and 4 CV.440s, although the latter are being phased out and replaced with more CV.580s.

The livery, designed by Gerald B. Hickman, Aspen's President, comes in 3 colour variations: some aircraft have white tops, orange cheatlines and "Aspen" in dark-blue (as illustrated); others have light-blue tops, orange cheatline and "Aspen" in white; and one aircraft (N4813C) has an orange top, light blue cheatline and "Aspen" in white. All 440s have dark-blue engines, while the 580 engines are in natural metal finish.

(Insignia — Plate 4)

27. ATHABASKA AIRWAYS

Athabaska Airways of Prince Albert, Saskatchewan, began operations in March 1955; and today offers both fixed-wing and helicopter services from its bases at Prince Albert, Lac la Ronge, Buffalo Narrows, Isle à la Crosse and Uranium City (all in Saskatchewan). Repair and maintenance facilities are operated, in addition.

Athabaska's current fleet numbers some 39 aircraft, including 2 Twin Otters, 2 Otters 2 Beavers, 1 Turbo Beaver and 13 helicopters.

The livery varies in detail between different types of aircraft, but is predominantly red (or red and maroon) on the helicopters; and light-blue, white and black on the fixed-wing aircraft. The Otters (as illustrated) have a white top and blue underside, divided by a black, trimmed cheatline; one Twin Otter (C-FCHE) is in a similar scheme, while the other (C-FWGE) has an all-white fuselage and a blue, black-trimmed cheat; and the Beavers have an all-white fuselage, a blue cheat and two matching horizontal blue bands across the top and centre of the white tail-fin. Most aircraft carry the airline titling in an attractive script form, and almost all have blue wing-tips.

(Insignia — Plate 2)

28. AUSTIN AIRWAYS

Austin Airways of Timmins, Ontario, was formed in 1934, and is the oldest contin-uously-operated airline in Canada. Today, scheduled flights serve the James Bay and Hudson Bay areas in Ontario and Quebec, while an extensive non-scheduled network covers communities in the Northwest Territories, Manitoba, northern Ontario and western Quebec. Austin offers, too, general passenger and cargo charters, aerial survey, forest fire patrol and aerial photography. The company was acquired in 1975 by the owners of White River Air Services, and the fleets are integrated, consisting of some 34 aircraft, including 4 DC-3s, 3 HS.748s, 3 Twin Otters, 5 Otters, 7 Beavers and a recently-acquired Cessna Citation.

Austin's standard livery is an extremely colourful one, being predominantly yellow, with a black, multi-trimmed cheatline. It is of note that, while many aircraft carry the title "Austin Airways Ltd" in white scripted lettering in the black cheatline, the HS.748s have — by tradition — no titling at all; and nor does the new Citation, illustrated here. Note also that the wings and horizontal tail stabilisers are yellow, too, on all aircraft using the standard scheme.

(Insignia — Plate 4)

25. Argosy's Douglas DC-3 N407D at Fort Lauderdale in April 1978. (Photograph by IAPS, J. Plaisier)

26. Aspen's Convair CV.440 N4814C at Sky Harbor on 29 May 1977.(Photograph by Ben Knowles, Jr.

27. Athabaska's de Havilland Canada DHC-3 Otter C-FZKW in May 1978.
(Photograph by John Kimberley)

28. Austin's Cessna Citation 500-1 C-GRQA at Toronto on 9 November 1978.
(Photograph by Russell Brown)

29. BAJA CORTEZ AIRLINES

Baja Cortez Airlines of Los Angeles offers scheduled passenger services between Los Angeles and the terminals of Mulege, Loreto, Alamos and Guaymas on Mexico's Baja California peninsula and western coast.

Two aircraft are used currently; a Riley Heron registered N690BC, and a PA-23 Aztec registered N6132Y.

The livery, as illustrated on the Heron, is extremely smart; with an all-white fuselage, wings and horizontal tail stabilisers. The main cheatline is in green, sweeping up to enclose the after-half of the tail-fin, while a thin red trimline runs the length of the green cheat, underneath it, and a heavier red trimline extends aft, tapering as it does so, from the red airline titles. Note also the gold "bird" motif on the fin, and the fact that the green cheat and red trimline are repeated on the aircraft's engines.

(Insignia — Plate 2)

30. BC YUKON AIR

BC Yukon Air Service of Watson Lake, Yukon, was formed in 1936 as Northern British Columbia Air Service, and took its present title in 1953. The airline operates both passenger and cargo flights within western Canada, and offers charter services in addition.

The current fleet consists of 6 aircraft: a Twin Otter, an Otter, a Beaver, an Islander and 2 Cessna 185s.

BC Yukon's livery, as illustrated, has an all-white fuselage with the main cheatline in red, and trimlines in red and dark-blue; and this theme is repeated on the aircraft engines. Note also the red rudder, and red aircraft registration — which is considerably larger than the black airline titling — and the red tips to wings and horizontal tail-stabilisers.

31. BONANZA AIRLINES

Bonanza Airlines of Las Vegas, Nevada, was formed in 1976 through the amalgamation of Monarch Aviation and Mountain West Airlines. Today, the airline operates scheduled services to link Las Vegas with Grand Junction and Aspen (both in Colorado) and Vail (Arizona); and currently proposes an Aspen-Dallas route. Extensive charter services are offered also from Las Vegas.

At the time of writing, at the end of 1978, Bonanza is awaiting CAB approval to operate F-27s; but the current fleet stands at 7 aircraft: a DC-3, a Gulfstream I and 5 Cessnas of mixed types.

Bonanza's livery is eye-catching, being largely white, but with a blue and green striped underside, and a double-cheatline which sits unusually high on the fuselage roof, and broadens as it moves aft to turn sharply up across the tail-fin. This cheatline, in matching blue and green stripes, embraces also the large black "B" motif on the fin. Note, too, that while the horizontal tail-stabilisers are in white, the engines and wings are left in a natural metal finish. Airline titling is in bold, black block letters above the passenger windows.

(Insignia — Plate 3)

32. BRADLEY AIR SERVICES

Bradley Air Services of Carp, Ontario, was formed in 1946 as the Bradley Flying School, but extended in the mid-1950s to undertake specialised charter and survey work in Arctic areas. This, in turn, has developed today into extensive charter operations from bases at Eureka, Frobisher Bay and Resolute (all in the Northwest Territories); while scheduled passenger services are conducted under the name of First Air (a Bradley subsidiary) to link Carp with Ottawa, Montreal, North Bay and Sudbury. Flying training is still offered, in addition, as are small aircraft sales and service.

The Bradley/First Air fleet consists of more than 20 aircraft, including 4 DC-3s, 7 Twin Otters, 3 Otters, 3 Beavers and 2 Beech 18s.

The livery, as illustrated, is not standard to all aircraft; although a black, or dark-green cheatline is generally favoured. On the Beech 18, this is augmented by bright-red tips to the wings, and a matching colour on the for'ard outer half of the tail-fins. Note also that, like Air-Dale and Austin, Bradley used the word "Ltd" in the airline titling.

(Insignia — Plates 2 & 3)

29. Baja Cortez's de Havilland DH.114 Riley Heron N690BC at Los Angeles in February 1978.
(Photograph by John Wegg)

30. BC Yukon's Britten-Norman BN-2A Islander C-GGYY in August 1978.
(Photograph by John Kimberley)

31.   Bonanza's Douglas DC-3 N101ZG in March 1978.   (Photograph from APS files)

32.   Bradley's Beech G18S C-FTAE in September 1977.   (Photograph by John Kimberley)

33. BRANIFF INTERNATIONAL AIRWAYS

Braniff International Airways of Dallas, Texas, was formed in 1928 and today operates over a route-network of some 29,000 miles in mainland USA, Hawaii, Mexico and South America. In addition, from March 1978, a B.747 service has been operated between Dallas/Fort Worth and London Gatwick.

The airline operates a fleet of over 100 aircraft, embracing 2 B.747s (one leased), 14 DC-8s and some 90 B.727s. It is likely, moreover, that shared Concorde operations will start early in 1979.

In April 1965, Braniff gained a new chairman, Harding L. Lawrence, who elected to dispense with a standard paint-scheme and to paint different aircraft in different colours — originally 7, and later 9, pastel shades — using an all-over scheme with white wings, fin and horizontal stabilisers. In 1971, coinciding with a fleet rational-isation, the variety was reduced to 4 two-tone colour schemes (orange/mustard, red/tan, green/olive, dark-blue/light-blue) with the upper colour continuing through the fin, and with bare metal wings and stabilisers. Later, in 1973 and 1975 respectively, came the now-famous DC-8 and B.727 in Alexander Calder's highly-original abstract schemes; and in Spring 1978, the current scheme — which introduces a new "overall" livery in a variety of main colours, offset by different trim colours, with the trim colour repeated in the new and attractive script-form of airline titling.

(Insignia — Plate 2)

34. BUFFALO AIRWAYS

Buffalo Airways operates both fixed-wing and helicopter services from its base at Fort Smith, some 150 miles south of the Great Slave Lake, in the Northwest Territories, using currently a fleet of 11 aircraft: an Otter, 2 Beavers, a PA-31 Navajo, 2 Cessna 185s, 2 Alouettes, 2 JetRangers and a Gazelle.

The livery, as illustrated, consists of an all-white fuselage, with a very broad dark-blue cheatline which becomes an anti-dazzle panel over the nose, and which tapers aft to the tail-unit. A thin red trimline runs above the cheatline, and a rather thicker one below, to the nose. The tail motif is a double-arrow arrangement in dark-blue and red; and note that the theme is repeated on the engines. Note also the red tips to the wings, the red aircraft registration, and the fact that in the airline titling, the word "Buffalo" is in script form, while the word "Airways" takes block letters.

(Insignia — Plate 3)

35. CANADIAN VOYAGEUR AIRLINES

Canadian Voyageur Airlines has its headquarters at Fort Frances, Ontario (close by the US border), and operates regular services from International Falls Municipal Airport to a number of terminals within the province. The airline holds authority, too, to conduct charter services out of Fort Frances.

Canadian Voyageur's current fleet numbers 7 aircraft: 2 Beavers, 2 Beech 18s, 2 Doves and a PA-23 Apache.

The livery, as illustrated, consists of an all-white fuselage, with a yellow, blue-trimmed nose-band which merges into cheat and trimlines in the same colours. The white wings carry wide yellow bands, with blue trim; and the blue and yellow logo is carried on the fin. Note also the yellow tips to the horizontal tail stabilisers, and the blue rim to the engine-cowling.

36. CAN-AIR SERVICES

Can-Air Services, with its headquarters at Edmonton, Alberta, operates passenger and freight charters throughout western Canada from its bases at St. Albert (Alberta), Vancouver (British Columbia) and Hay River in the Northwest Territories. The airline has 2 PBY-5A Cansos and a DC-3; and most recently, one Canso (CF-DIL) has been at Vancouver, the other (CF-SAT) has been at Hay River, and the DC-3 (C-GWZS) has been home-based. All aircraft are used widely, however, and may move between bases as required.

The DC-3 does not wear titles, but the 2 Cansos do; although they are in different schemes. CF-SAT, as illustrated, is in a silver finish overall, with a red cheatline and red tips to the wings. CF-DIL, recently repainted, has a cheatline similar to CF-SAT's but is white overall, with red engines and wing-tips. Both Cansos carry the airline titling in the cheatline for'ard.

33. Braniff's Boeing 727-227 N412BN in a brown and cream version of the new livery, in April 1978.
(Photograph by W.C. Wann, Jr.)

34. Buffalo's Piper PA-31 Navajo CF-CSD in October 1977. (Photograph by John Kimberley)

35.   Canadian Voyageur's de Havilland Canada DHC-2 Beaver C-FOCX in August 1976.
(Photograph by Phil Hanson)

36.   Can-Air's Consolidated PBY-5A Canso CF-SAT in November 1976.(Photograph by John Kimberley)

37. CAPITAL AIR SURVEYS

Capital Air Surveys of Killaloe, Ontario, offers a variety of services in the field of aerial survey/photography, using a fleet of 11 aircraft: 2 Beech 3NMs, a Beech 3TM, a DC-3, a Helio Courier, a Learjet and 5 PA-23s.

Capital Air Surveys' aircraft operate in several livery forms, although a theme of red and white is generally favoured: for instance, the Courier has a white upper fuselage and a red underside, with a thin black cheatline, and red wing-tips and propeller-boss; while the Learjet is white overall, with a red cheatline and a red stripe on the outboard side of the wing-tanks. The Beech 3s are in a standard livery, however, as illustrated: with a white upper fuselage and red underside, and thin black cheatline (all reminiscent of the Courier); and red wings, engines and tail-fins. The white "arrow" shape on the tail-fins is also standard; as are the black and white stripes on the engines.

38. CARIBBEAN AIR SERVICES

Caribbean Air Services was known until 1969 as Virgin Island Airways, having been formed in 1962 as an air-taxi service. Today, however, the airline operates cargo-only services from its base at St. Croix (US Virgin Islands) to various Caribbean destinations, including Puerto Rico, St. Lucia, St. Kitts, Antigua and Haiti.

The airline is now one of the largest remaining users of the venerable C-46 (the Curtiss Commando of World War II fame), having a fleet of six.

Airline titling, when worn, is abbreviated on the aircraft to "CASAIR" and is in red, as is the cheatline. The airline's president, Mr. John Stuart-Jervis states that the "bird" motif was designed to "avoid too much clutter on the tail"; and certainly, the simple livery complements the lines of the C-46 and the overall impression is a clean, smart and business-like one. Note that not all aircraft wear the airline title; and that, in the company logo (although, again, not always on the aircraft), the central "beak" of the bird is in orange, while the "wings" are in red.

(Insignia — Plate 1)

39. CATALINA AIRLINES

Catalina Airlines of San Pedro, California, operates high-frequency commuter services between the Californian mainland (ie, its main base at San Pedro, and Long Beach Airport) and the Pebbly Beach Air Terminal on Santa Catalina Island, a celebrated holiday and tourist resort. The airline has been serving Catalina since 1953; and was formerly Avalon Air Transport, taking its current title in July 1963.

Having absorbed the fleet and operations of Air Catalina at the beginning of 1978, the airline has now seven Grumman Goose amphibians (operating from San Pedro only) and up to four helicopters, used seasonally (operating both from San Pedro and Long Beach), to cover the 32-mile route.

On amalgamating with Air Catalina, Catalina Airlines adopted a new livery for the Goose aircraft (bringing them more into line, in fact, with the helicopters). Gone is the old cream, green and brown scheme, and the aircraft are now white overall; with dark-blue engines, and blue, red and white stripes running aft along the length of the aircraft from a small "goose's head" symbol near the nose. Note that airline titling, in small red block letters set into the main red stripe, appears on the port (ie door) side of the aircraft only; and that the logo on the tail-fin is also new.

(Insignia — Plate 1)

40. CHALK'S INTERNATIONAL AIRLINE

Chalk's International Airline of Miami, Florida, is probably the oldest continuously-operated airline in the USA, for records show that it was formed — as Chalk's Flying Service — in 1919. Today, the airline offers scheduled seaplane services between Miami and destinations in the Bahamas (including Nassau); and additionally operates passenger charter services throughout the Bahamas.

Chalk's fleet consists of 5 Mallards, all in a smart livery of white overall, with orange cheatline and floats, and dark-blue engines. Note, however, that the stylised airline titling on the nose can be in two forms: as "Chalk International" (eg N3010) and as "Chalk's International", ie using the possessive, as in the airline's usual business title (eg N2970). In both forms, nonetheless, the design of the logo is identical, with the word "International" set into the tail of the "C" in the company name.

(Insignia — Plate 2)

37. Capital Air Surveys' Beech 3NM CF-SUQ in July 1977.   (Photograph by John Kimberley)

38. Caribbean Air Services' Curtiss C-46D N609SE in March 1976.   (Photograph by Herbert Kraft)

39.   Catalina's Grumman G.21A Goose N322 at Pebbly Beach on 20 May 1978.

(Photograph by the author)

40.   Chalk's Grumman G.73 Mallard N2970 in September 1977.

(Photograph from author's private collection)

41. CHAPARRAL AIRLINES

Chaparral Airlines of Abilene, Texas, was formed on 11 August 1975, and commenced operations on 15 September 1976. It is an intra-state carrier, linking Abilene by scheduled services with Austin, Dallas (Love Field), Houston, Lubbock and Midland/Odessa. Charters are also undertaken, as is a small-parcels air-freight service.

The current fleet consists of 3 Navajo Chieftains, registered N12CA, N17CA and N39CA.

Chaparral's livery is such that the author may be forgiven for referring the reader to the colour photograph, rather than attempting to describe it! Certainly, the white, ochre and brown colour-scheme can be called "eye-catching"; and is refreshing in its originality. Note that while the airline titling is relatively small, the registration is in bold characters on the lower after fuselage.

42. COCHISE AIRLINES

Cochise Airlines of Tucson, Arizona, was formed in September 1971 and operates scheduled services within its home state, linking Tucson with Winslow, Yuma, Douglas, Flagstaff, Grand Canyon, Phoenix, Prescott and other terminals. The airline can offer also charter services to different areas, and into Mexico; and undertakes in addition aerial tours of the Grand Canyon National Park.

Cochise's current fleet consists of 2 Cessna 402Bs, plus a Twin Otter leased from Key Airlines.

The Cessnas are painted in a smart white, orange and brown livery, with the logo displayed on the orange, upper section of the tail-fin, and with airline titles in rather small, two-coloured lettering beneath. Note also the variety of trimlines used in the scheme, including the thin white line between the orange and brown components of the double-cheat. The leased Twin Otter is in a mixed livery, having Cochise titles on the for'ard fuselage, but with the Key logo on an all-white tail.

(Insignia — Plate 3)

43.   COMMAND AIRWAYS

Command Airways of Wappingers Falls, near Poughkeepsie in New York State, began operations in 1966. Today, the airline undertakes scheduled commuter services in New York State and New England; serving both La Guardia and Kennedy Airports in New York City, Poughkeepsie, Binghampton and White Plains in New York state, Burlington in Vermont and Boston and Pittsfield in Massachusetts.

Command was the first US airline to order the Shorts 330 wide-bodied commuter aircraft; and currently operates two, plus two Beech 99s and two Twin Otters.

The livery, as illustrated, is smart but simple, in keeping with the lines of the Shorts 330; and consists essentially of an all-white fuselage with a double-cheatline in dark-blue and bright red, tapered at the nose but sweeping aft to broaden out and up to the tail, with matching stripes on the tail-fins. Cheatline colours are repeated in the "anti-dazzle panel position" for'ard of the flight-deck windows, in broad "V" shapes. Note, too, that the engines are left in natural metal finish, on white wings.

(Insignia — Plate 3)

44.   CONAIR AVIATION

Conair Aviation of Abbotsford, British Columbia, was formed in 1969; and today operates a variety of services, embracing charter work, forestry and agricultural contracts, fire control, crop-spraying and dusting, seeding and fertilizing, and oil-spillage control. These services are carried out primarily in British Columbia and the Northwest Territories.

Conair's current fleet numbers some 40 aircraft, including 7 DC-6Bs, 13 Douglas A-26C Invaders, 8 Grumman TBM3E Avengers and 4 Aerostar 600s.

Conair's livery varies between different types of aircraft, but is essentially in a white and red theme; with red fleet numbers carried on the tail-fins of the larger aircraft. The DC-6B, as illustrated, carries the title "Conair Aviation"; but most of the fleet has the word "Conair" only, often with the capital letter "C" enlarged and off-set to form a kind of crescent around the rest of the word. Note also that some of the Avengers have dayglo paint on tail-fin and wing-tips.

(Insignia — Plate 4)

41.   Chaparral's Piper PA-31 Navajo Chieftain N39CA at Dallas (Love Field) on 3 April 1978.
(Photograph by Terry Chamberlin)

42.   Cochise's Cessna 402B N5407M at Tucson on 27 November 1975.
(Photograph by Ben Knowles, Jr.)

43.   Command's Shorts 330 N51DD at East Midlands Airport, England in June 1976, prior to delivery
to the USA.   (Photograph from author's private collection)

44.   Conair's Douglas DC-6B C-GIOY in August 1978.   (Photograph by John Kimberley)

45. CONTACT AIRWAYS

Contact Airways of Fort McMurray, Alberta, was formed in January 1961; and today operates a variety of charter and air-taxi services, to link its base with small and often remote communities in far-flung regions. The airline undertakes also low-level environmental surveys, and air-ambulance flights.

Contact's current fleet consists of 11 aircraft, including 3 PA-23 Aztecs, 3 Cessna 185s, a DC-3, a Dornier Do28-B1 and a PA-31 Navajo.

The livery consists essentially of an all-white fuselage, with a broad pale-yellow cheatline trimmed in white and black. The black and yellow "wedge" shape worn on the tail-fin is standard to most aircraft, although in the case of some (eg, the DC-3), it is "clean"; while on others (eg, the Navajo, as illustrated), it bears a small oval airline symbol. The airline titles, in styled block letters as illustrated, are also generally standard. Note, however, that some of the smaller aircraft do not keep to the standard livery: eg, the Do-28-B1 has a white upper fuselage and tail, a black cheatline (and a parallel line across the tail-fin), and pale-yellow underside, engines and wings; with small, non-standard titles set into the cheatline.

(Insignia — Plate 2)

46. CONTINENTAL AIRLINES

Continental Airlines of Los Angeles, California, has roots in Varney Speed Lines, which began operations in 1926. In 1930, Varney was bought by United Airlines (qv); but the southwest division of Varney reformed outside United in 1934, to become Varney Air Transport — changing its name to Continental Air Lines on 1 July 1937. Today, Continental is one of the major carriers in the USA, with a route network which, fittingly, spans the continent. Services are operated also to Honolulu; and in conjunction with Continental's affiliate, Air Micronesia, from Honolulu, Guam and Okinawa to the US Pacific Islands Trust Territory, and onwards to Tokyo.

From 1970 to 1975, Continental operated 4 B.747s, but a rationalisation has now reduced the fleet to two basic types: the DC-10-10 and the B.727; numbers being currently at 14 DC-10s, 36 B.727-200s and 8 B.727-100s.

Continental's current livery was introduced in 1968 — the year in which the airline became an all-fan-jet operator — and is most striking. The triple cheatline is in orange, red and gold, with a sweep to a gold fin which bears the logo in black. With the livery change, the airline titling was shortened from "Continental Airlines" to "Continental" — and is now flanked by a smaller gold version of the logo, and the US flag.

(Insignia — Plate 3)

47. COUGAR AIR

Cougar Air has its headquarters at Victoria Airport in Sidney, British Columbia, and offers services with a small fleet of 5 aircraft: a PA-23 Aztec, a Cessna 180 on floats, and 3 Helio Couriers, also on floats.

The livery on the Aztec, as illustrated, is in fact the colours of the aircraft's former owner, the now-defunct Victoria Flying Services: a white upper fuselage and orange underside and tail areas, separated by a double and curved cheatline in green and yellow. The wings are also in orange, with the engines in white, and Cougar Air titles — in black and reading "Cougar Air — Victoria, BC" — have been added, with a stylised cougar's head in outline. The blue and white "sailing ship" badge worn in the photograph is a shield used by British Columbia-based aircraft in 1978, to celebrate a bicentennial of the explorer Captain Cook. The shield carries the words "Captain Cook Bicentennial British Columbia Canada" and the dates "1778-1978".

(Insignia — Plate 4)

48. CP AIR

CP Air, with its head office at Vancouver International Airport, British Columbia, was formed on 30 January 1942 as Canadian Pacific Airlines, when Canadian Pacific Railways acquired and unified ten small bush operators. The airline tooks its current name in 1968 and today, flies a lengthy domestic route-network from Vancouver, Edmonton, Calgary, Winnipeg, Toronto, Ottawa and Montreal. International services reach several points in Europe; Lima, Buenos Aires and Santiago in South America; Mexico City; San Francisco, Los Angeles and Honolulu; Fiji; and Sydney, Tokyo and Hong Kong in the East.

CP Air's current fleet consists of 25 aircraft: 4 B.747s, 12 DC-8s, 2 B.727-200s and 7 B.737-200s. A further 3 B.737s and 4 DC-10-30s are presently on order.

The livery is distinctive; with an orange upper fuselage and metal underside, divided by a broad red diagonal cheatline. The company logo — an irregular red right-angled triangle within an irregular white "semi-circle" — is worn boldly on the tail-fin; and B.747s and DC-8s carry an aircraft name: the B.747s have names of nations — eg "Empress of Japan", "Empress of Australia" — while the DC-8s have names of cities — eg "Empress of Honolulu", "Empress of Lisbon". Note also the simple black airline titling, worn on the nose.

(Insignia — Plate 3)

45. Contact's Piper PA-31 Navajo CF-ZOW in May 1977.   (Photograph by John Kimberley)

46. Continental's McDonnell Douglas DC-10-10CF N68049 "Robert F. Six" on approach in October
1978.   (Photograph by John Kimberley)

47. Cougar Air's Piper PA-23 Aztec C-FUCJ at Vancouver on 11 July 1978.
(Photograph by K. Simpson)

48. CP Air's McDonnell Douglas DC-8-43 CF-CPJ "Empress of Mexico City" at Toronto on 16 June 1978.
(Photograph by Russell Brown)

49. DELTA AIR LINES

Delta Air Lines of Atlanta, Georgia, was formed in 1925 as the world's first airborne crop-dusting service, and began passenger flights in 1929. These passenger flights were discontinued in 1930 (the company went back to crop-dusting) but were resumed in 1934. The company merged with Chicago and Southern Air Lines in 1953, and with Northeast in 1972. Today, Delta ranks as one of the world's largest passenger-carrying airlines: international routes reach Canada, Jamaica, Bermuda, the Bahamas, Puerto Rico, Venezuela and — since May 1978 — London Gatwick: while domestic routes reach most of the Eastern and Midwest states, and extend to the Southwest and California.

Delta's current fleet consists of 193 aircraft: 25 L-1011s, 23 DC-8s, 92 B.727-200s and 53 DC-9-30s. A further 7 L-1011s (5 of them, L-1011-500s) and 30-plus B.727s are on order.

The name "Delta" is taken from the Mississippi delta, while the Greek letter delta, for "D", is the origin of the logo. Within the company, the logo is known as "the widget" (origin of that unknown!) and credit for its design is shared by the airline's engineering department and furnishing section, and the advertising agency Burke Dowling Adams. Note that a small version of the widget is set into the dark-blue cheatline, for'ard; that even smaller widgets appear on the engine-pods; and that a red trimline runs between the upper edge of the cheat and the airline titles, and extends the length of the aircraft.

(Insignia — Plate 3)

50. EASTERN AIRLINES

Eastern Airlines, with its head office at Miami International Airport, has its origins in Pitcairn Aviation, a mail-carrier which began services over a New York - Atlanta route in 1928. From these small beginnings, Eastern has grown into a major operator; serving 28 states in the US, plus the District of Columbia, and having international routes to Canada, Mexico, Bermuda, the Bahamas and the Caribbean. In addition, Eastern operates an "air-shuttle" — an hourly-service, guaranteed-seating-without-reservation scheme — linking New York and Washington DC, and New York and Boston.

Eastern's current fleet stands at 248 aircraft: 31 L-1011s, 4 A300B4 Airbuses, 53 B.727-200s, 70 B.727-100s and 90 DC-9s. Further Tristars, Airbuses and B.727s are on order.

In early 1977, Eastern re-introduced a "great silver fleet" theme, whereby its aircraft have gone into an all-metal finish on fuselage and tail, while retaining the distinctive "hockey-stick" or double-cheatline, in two tones of blue: the lighter blue is termed "Caribbean", and the darker "Ionosphere". The company logo, worn adjacent to the titles, in white on a blue field, is in fact a stylised "falcon". Note that the A300 Airbuses have not taken the new livery (they have an all-white fuselage, with the double-cheatline) because of the special anti-corrosive paint in which these aircraft are supplied; and that the latest batch of DC-9s delivered (of which N407EA, illustrated here, is one) have cheatlines, titles and logo "picked out" attractively in white trim.

(Insignia — Plate 3)

51. EASTERN PROVINCIAL AIRWAYS

Eastern Provincial Airways of Gander, Newfoundland, was formed in 1949, and began scheduled services in 1950. Today, EPA's route-network covers Montreal and the Magdalen Islands in Quebec; Charlottetown on Prince Edward Island; Charlo, Chatham, Fredericton, Moncton and St. John in New Brunswick; Halifax and Sydney in Nova Scotia; and Churchill Falls, Deer Lake, Gander, Goose Bay, St. John's, Stephenville and Wabush in Newfoundland.

EPA's current fleet consists of 6 B.737-200s and 2 HS.748s.

The simple red and white livery is dominated by the logo on the tail-fin, which is an Atlantic sea gull in full flight and which — to quote the airline — is "known for its tenacity, diligence, superb flying qualities, and friendliness; and symbolizes both the Atlantic provinces of Canada and the sleek, graceful conquest of the coastal skies". Note also that the cheatline ends aft in a wedge-shape, just for'ard of the tail-unit, and that airline titles are in a slightly-stylised form of block lettering.

(Insignia — Plate 3)

52. ELDORADO AVIATION

Eldorado Aviation of Edmonton, Alberta, offers both passenger and freight services, principally for Eldorado Nuclear Ltd and the Northern Transportation Company. In addition, the airline undertakes survey-work, and ice and power-line patrols.

Eldorado's fleet consists of 2 DC-4s, 2 DC-3s and 4 helicopters — a Sikorsky S-55 and 3 Bell 47Gs.

The livery, as illustrated, is new to C-FJRW in 1978, brings it to conformity with the other DC-4, C-FGNI, and thus may be regarded as the standard scheme. The double-cheatline in red and dark-blue sweeps up through the tail-fin and lends relief to what is otherwise a very simple livery. Note, however, that C-FGNI has a light-grey underside, instead of polished metal, and carries the words "Eldorado Aviation Limited" in very small letters beneath the cheatline for'ard, in addition to the bold main title in mid-fuselage.

49. Delta's McDonnell Douglas DC-8-51 N818E at San Francisco on 25 May 1978.

(Photograph by the author)

50. Eastern's McDonnell Douglas DC-9-51 N407EA at Toronto in October 1978.

(Photograph by Gary Vincent)

51.   Eastern Provincial's Boeing 737-2E1 C-FEPP in January 1977.   (Photograph by Bruce Drum)

52.   Eldorado's Douglas DC-4 C-FJRW in May 1978.   (Photograph by John Kimberley)

53. EVERGREEN INTERNATIONAL AIRLINES

Evergreen International Airlines of Marana, Arizona, was formerly Johnson Flying Service, in which name it operated until 1975, when it became a subsidiary of Evergreen Helicopters Inc. As Johnson Flying Service, the airline had been in existence since 1924, and was given one of the first US supplemental-carrier certificates in 1957. Evergreen operates throughout the continental United States, and to Alaska, Hawaii and Canada. Expanded authority to fly to the Caribbean and Mexico is in course of ratification. In addition, the airline undertakes charters, contracts for the military and the US Forestry Service, and a host of similar commitments and programmes.

Evergreen's expansion in 1976 into the all-cargo charter market brought with it an increased fleet, which stands currently at 5 DC-8s, 3 DC-9s, 2 Electras, 4 CV.580Fs, a C-46, 2 DC-3s and 3 light aircraft.

In simple and effective styling, the livery is highlighted by a circle of six 5-pointed stars, embracing both cheatlines (which are in two values of green) aft of the flight-deck windows. Triple bands, in the same two shades of green, adorn the tail-fin. Note, too, the styling of the letter "E" in what is otherwise a standard block-capital form of airline titling.

(Insignia — Plate 3)

54. FALCON AIRWAYS

Falcon Airways of Addison, Texas, operates all-cargo services which link Dallas and Houston in Texas; Little Rock in Arkansas; Atlanta in Georgia; Chicago in Illinois; Memphis in Tennessee; and New Orleans, Patterson, Houma, Lake Charles and Lafayette in Louisiana.

Falcon's fleet consists of 2 DC-4s, 4 DC-3s, a Beech 3NM, a Beech TC-45J and a Dove.

The principal component of the livery is a triple-cheatline, in dark-blue, white and light-blue, which runs from the tip of the nose along the length of the aircraft and up into the tail-fin, to embrace there a black stylised falcon, which is the company logo (and which faces forward always on the aircraft). The DC-4s are ex-USAF and were operating in mid-1978 without airline titles or cheatlines; but in military colours of white upper fuselage and light-grey underside, and with ownership of the aircraft being marked only by application of the falcon logo on the fin.

(Insignia — Plate 4)

55. FEDERAL EXPRESS

Federal Express of Memphis, Tennessee, was formed in 1972 and is a privately-owned airline, operating a charter service for small packages and freight, to more then 135 cities in the USA (including Alaska) and to Toronto, Canada. Three standards of service are offered — all of them guaranteeing delivery by a specified time — with many flights taking place overnight.

Until late 1977, Federal Express used almost exclusively a fleet of cargo-converted Falcon 20s, with a specially-fitted 74" x 60" cargo-door. Then, however, with the acquisition of authority to operate larger aircraft, the airline took on additionally a pair of B.727-100Cs, to expand the network. The current fleet stands, thus, at 32 Falcon 20s and 2 B.727-100Cs, with a further 5 B.727s and 25 stretched Canadair Challengers on order.

The livery was introduced on the first of Federal Express's Falcons (N8FE), is carried additionally on the company's vans, was created by Richard Runyon Design of Los Angeles, and is a striking combination of purple, white and orange, with the airline titling displayed boldly across almost a third of the aircraft's length. All Falcons have a girl's name, while the company calls itself "the small package airline".

(Insignia — Plate 2)

56. FLEMING INTERNATIONAL AIRWAYS

Fleming International Airways of Pompano Beach, Florida, specialises in cargo-charter and is well-established, with services throughout the United States. Among enthusiasts, the airline is further celebrated for its continued championing and use of the DC-7, being one of the last US airlines to keep the type in service.

Currently, Fleming International has one DC-7 (N356AL) and two Electras (N666F and N667F).

The livery is simple, consisting essentially of a white upper fuselage, with a plain white tail-fin, a metal-finish underside and a broad orange cheatline. It is of note, however, that while airline titling is normally in black, Electra N667F (the latest aircraft, acquired in late 1977) wears orange titles to match the cheatline, and has these placed rather more "amidships" on the fuselage than is normal practice.

53. Evergreen's McDonnell Douglas DC-8-52 N800EV on 17 November 1976.

(Photograph by Ben Knowles, Jr.)

54. Falcon's Douglas DC-3 N85FA in January 1978. (Photograph from author's private collection)

55.   Federal Express's Dassault Falcon 20DC N37FE "Theresa" in January 1976.
(Photograph from author's private collection)

56.   Fleming International's Douglas DC-7C/F N356AL at Miami in December 1976.
(Photograph by Bruce Drum)

57. FLORIDA AIRLINES

Florida Airlines of Sarasota, Florida, began operations in its current name and form in 1968, a year after Air South of St. Simons Island, Georgia. The two airlines merged in 1975, to offer scheduled commuter and cargo services which link Miami, Sarasota/Bradenton, Fort Lauderdale, Fort Myers and Tampa in Florida; Atlanta and St. Simons Island in Georgia; and Hilton Head in South Carolina.

The current fleet consists of 7 DC-3s and a Martin 404, the last being acquired in the fall of 1978.

Most, but not all, of Florida Airlines' aircraft wear still the unusual form of airline titling stemming from the integration with Air South; and the livery is colourful, with a white upper fuselage, a mustard underside and a double-cheatline in two values of red. Note also the white engines.

(Insignia — Plates 2 & 3)

58. FLYING FIREMAN

The Flying Fireman Ltd., based at Victoria International Airport in Sidney, British Columbia, is a company flying mainly within western Canada, and offering forest protection services and aerial fire-control, with Canso water-bombers which are fitted out fully for fire-fighting.

The current fleet consists of 6 Cansos and 3 Cessna T337Gs, which are the turbo-system variant of the twin-boomed Super Skymaster.

The livery, as illustrated, consists of an all-silver finish, but for red tips to the wings and the horizontal tail-stabilisers, and a red underside to the Canso's "hull". Note also the black anti-dazzle panel on the nose, the fleet number for'ard and the stylised letter "Y" in the airline titling, which is in fact the standard form of the company logo.

(Insignia — Plate 3)

59. FLYING TIGERS

The Flying Tiger Line of Los Angeles, California, was the first all-cargo airline in the USA, having been formed in June 1945 as the National Skyway Freight Corporation. The airline took its current name in 1946, and is today the world's largest all-cargo air carrier, providing a daily scheduled service across the continental United States, and on across the Pacific to Japan, Taiwan, Korea, Hong Kong and the Philippines. In addition, the airline undertakes worldwide cargo charters and US military contracts.

The airline operates with two basic types only — the B.747 and the DC-8 — and the current fleet stands at 4 B.747-100Fs, 14 DC-8-63CFs and 7 DC-8-61s.

Traditionally, Flying Tigers aircraft carry horizontal blue stripes on the fuselage, running the length of the aircraft; a tradition established in 1947 with C-54s. Generally, the DC-8s still carry the stripes, but the B.747s were introduced in 1974 with a revised design incorporating white, red and blue diagonal stripes around the fuselage. A further change in May 1977 replaced the old "Circle T" insignia on the tail-fin with the bold white slanted lettering now common both to DC-8s and B.747s. Although most Flying Tigers aircraft have an all-silver finish, some are flying in 1978 with white-topped fuselages (eg N860FT as illustrated, and DC-8-63CF N871TV). (Insignia — Plate 3)

60. FRONTIER AIRLINES

Frontier Airlines of Denver, Colorado, can trace its history back to 1946, to Monarch Airlines, a Denver local service operator. In 1949, Monarch acquired Challenger Airlines, and then Arizona Airways in April 1950; and in June 1950, changed its name to Frontier Airlines. Frontier, in turn, acquired Central Airlines of Fort Worth, Texas, on 1 October 1967. Today, Frontier is one of the largest regional carriers in the USA, serving more than 100 cities in 16 states, and with international routes from Las Vegas and Kansas City, through Denver, to Winnipeg in Canada.

Frontier's current fleet stands at 52 aircraft: 22 B.737-200s, 27 CV.580s and 3 Twin Otters. A further 10 B.737s are on order.

The latest livery, introduced in February 1978 and designed by Saul Bass and Associates of Los Angeles, puts a striking combination of red, orange and burgundy stripes on to an all-white fuselage, and replaces the old "bow and arrow" logo with a stylised "F" symbol — featured both on the tail-fin and on the fuselage adjacent to the airline titling. Note, too, that while the B.737s and CV.580s wear the titles conventionally above the cheatlines, the Twin Otters — because of the high wing — have theirs beneath. (Insignia — Plate 2)

57. Florida Airlines' Douglas DC-3 N21768 in January 1978.   (Photograph by George Kinney)

58. Flying Fireman's Consolidated PBY-5A Canso C-GFFC "Lady M" in May 1978.
(Photograph by John Kimberley)

59. Flying Tigers' McDonnell Douglas DC-8-63CF N860FT at Los Angeles on 21 May 1978.
(Photograph by the author)

60. Frontier's de Havilland Canada DHC-6 Twin Otter N983FL in June 1978.
(Photograph by John Kimberley)

61.   GATEWAY AVIATION

Gateway Aviation of Edmonton, Alberta, was formed in June 1952, and offers passenger and cargo charters mainly within Alberta, the Northwest Territories and the Arctic islands. A scheduled service connects Rainbow Lake, Peace River, Slave Lake and the Jasper National Park with Edmonton; and support services are undertaken, too, for the Government and the oil, mining and other industries.

The current fleet totals 21 aircraft: 4 DC-3s, an HS.748, 4 Twin Otters, an MU-2, 2 Cessna 402s, 2 Cessna 310s, a Cessna 337, a Cessna 185, 2 Cessna 172s and 3 Otters.

Essentially, the livery consists of a red cheatline, a red triangular "G" logo and red airline titling; but where the Twin Otters, the Cessna 402s and the MU-2 have all-white fuselages, the DC-3s, the HS.748 and the Otters are light-grey beneath the cheatline. The smaller Cessnas are in non-standard livery and do not necessarily repeat the red and white theme — eg, Cessna 310 CF-GAT is blue and white — and some have the airline titles in white, set into the colour of the cheatline.

(Insignia — Plate 1)

62.   GLEN AIR SERVICES

Glen Air Services is based at Fort Nelson, in north-east British Columbia (not to be confused with the town of Nelson, in the southern part of the province and almost due east of Vancouver). The airline offers a full range of charter passenger services, on an "any time, any place" basis, limited only by the range of its fleet.

This fleet consists of 2 aircraft, both Cessna 185s; registered CF-NTM and CF-YOP.

The livery, as illustrated, consists of a white upper fuselage and an orange-red underside; and this orange-red colour is carried also on the top of the fin and at the tips of the white wings. A thin white, black-trimmed cheatline runs the length of the aircraft and is repeated on the orange-red part of the fin. Airline titling is worn on the fuselage waist, in black scripted form; and in very small block capitals beneath are the words "Ft. Nelson, BC".

63. GOLDEN WEST AIRLINES

Golden West Airlines of Newport Beach, California, was formed in 1968 to provide fast and efficient transportation between Los Angeles International and outlying airports; and today, is one of the largest commuter airlines in the USA, linking Los Angeles with a large number of terminals throughout southern California, including Inyokern, Palmdale, Mohave, Ontario, Riverside, Fullerton, Santa Ana, Oxnard and Santa Barbara. Other services link San Diego with Orange County, Oxnard and Santa Barbara.

The Golden West fleet consists of 14 aircraft: 12 Twin Otters and 2 Shorts 330s, acquired in 1977.

The livery changed at the end of 1976; and although the new scheme followed the same basic lines of the old, there were striking colour changes. The old red and ochre cheatline combination was replaced with bolder shades of mustard-yellow and dark-brown; and the old "clock" sunburst motif on the tail-fin was changed to a "half-sun" sign which is the airline's current logo. Note that the cheatline colours are repeated around the tail-fin logo, and that the engines are in dark-brown.

(Insignia — Plate 2)

64. GOLFE AIR QUEBEC

Golfe Air Quebec of Hauterive, Quebec, was known formerly as Baie Comeau Air Services; and today, still links Baie Comeau with Rimouski, Forestville and Mont Joli, by scheduled passenger service. Non-scheduled and charter operations are undertaken, too, from the above-named terminals.

The current fleet consists of 3 DC-3s, a Trislander, 2 Islanders, a Beech 18 and a Beaver.

Golfe Air's red and white livery varies slightly between types of aircraft inasmuch as the Trislander (as illustrated) takes the lower cheatline up into the after part of the tail-fin; while the Islanders have two "straight-through" red cheatlines on the white fuselage, and an all-red fin. Standard, however, is the "gold disc" logo and note that, in the stylised "G" therein, the horizontal bar is in fact an aircraft shape. Note, too, that on the aircraft, the company name is run into one word, with the "e" deleted, in the form "Golfair".

(Insignia — Plate 4)

61.	Gateway's Mitsubishi MU-2B-30 CF-AXP at the airline's main base in June 1976.
(Photograph by John Kimberley)

62.	Glen Air Services' Cessna 185 CF-NTM in June 1977.	(Photograph by John Kimberley)

63.   Golden West's de Havilland Canada DHC-6 Twin Otter N66200 at Los Angeles on 21 May 1978.
(Photograph by the author)

64.   Golfe Air's Britten-Norman BN-2A Trislander CF-CHZ in November 1975.
(Photograph by Bruce Drum)

65. GREAT LAKES AIRLINES

Great Lakes Airlines of London, Ontario, was formed in 1960 as the air transport section of the Holmes Blunt Company, and took the name Great Lakes Air Services in 1961, when charter operations were started. In 1967, when scheduled intra-province (Ontario) services began, the name changed again to the current title. Ownership of the airline passed in 1975 to the Hatch-Plaxton Company; and today, Great Lakes offers scheduled daily passenger services to link Sarnia, London and Toronto; and weekday-only services to Toronto-Peterborough-Ottawa. Charter operations are also undertaken.

Great Lakes has a current fleet of 4 CV.580s; but it is understood that 2 F-28s may be acquired in 1979.

Over the years, a number of liveries have appeared on Great Lakes' aircraft; notably one with a logo which was a map of the Great Lakes themselves, and another which had a stylised grouping of the letters "GLA". The current scheme is, however, more streamlined; with a triple-cheatline in brown and orange, which tapers to the nose in a form of "speed-wedge", and the current logo — on the tail-fin — is an echo of the same.

(Insignia — Plate 1)

66. GREAT NORTHERN AIRLINES

Great Northern Airlines of Fairbanks, Alaska, can trace back its history to 1946, and was known formerly as Fairbanks Air Service; taking its current title in October 1975. Today, the airline offers passenger services to Anchorage, Clear, Healy, McKinley, Nenana, Summit, Talkteena and Usibelli; and operates also an air-taxi and rental service, and a flying school.

The current fleet consists of 8 aircraft: 5 C-46s and 3 Electras.

The Great Northern livery comprises essentially an all-yellow fuselage offset by twin cheatlines in brown. The upper cheatline is foreshortened to accommodate the airline titles, while both are broken in the upward sweep across the tail-fin, such that each houses a letter of the "GN" on the upper fin. Note also the yellow bosses on the propellers, and the black-anti-dazzle panel on the nose.

(Insignia — Plate 1)

67. GULF-AIR AVIATION

Gulf-Air Aviation of Campbell River, Vancouver Island, British Columbia, was
known formerly as Trans Mountain Air Services, and took its current title in 1976,
the better to reflect its coastal operations. Services from Campbell River link Bute
Inlet, Knight Inlet, Loughborough Inlet, Kingcome Inlet and Alert Bay; and other
stops are made at the many small logging-camps and fishing-villages along the coast.
Charter and freight services are also undertaken.

The fleet has expanded since Trans Mountain days, and consists now of 2 Twin
Otters, 3 Otters, a Beaver, an Islander and 4 small Cessnas. All aircraft, other than
the Islander and one Cessna, are float-equipped.

The livery is essentially that inherited from Trans Mountain: an all-white fuselage
with green cheatline, green leading-edges to wings and horizontal stabilisers, green
wing-tips and a black band on the upper fin, housing the white aircraft registration.
Gulf-Air titles and motif have been applied; and it is of note that the motif is based
on the Great Thunderbird, a legendary creation of the coastal Indians. At present,
one aircraft — Twin Otter CF-IOH — wears a non-standard scheme, with a red cheatline and trim.

(Insignia — Plate 1)

68. HAIDA AIRLINES

Haida Airlines, based at Vancouver Harbour, British Columbia, was incorporated in
1976, in which year the company acquired its principal operating subsidiary, Island
Airlines (qv). In 1977, Haida took over in addition the licences of Airspan Flight
Charter. The result is that, between them, Haida and Island Air now fly scheduled
services to link Vancouver and Campbell River with Victoria, Comox, Gold River,
Tahsis, Kyuquot, Toba, Cortes and Powell River. Charter services include aerial
inspection, reconnaisance, advertising and sightseeing.

The combined Haida and Island Air fleet comprises 22 aircraft: a Goose, an Islander,
an Otter, 6 Beavers and 13 small Cessnas.

The livery illustrated is perhaps the most attractive of the many variations worn by
Haida and Island Air aircraft, which can be held to be generally interchangeable
between the two airlines, who alter titles and logos as necessary (and sometimes,
indeed, aircraft wear both logos at once). Beaver C-FGYK is clearly a Haida aircraft,
however, with the distinctive logo on fuselage and tail-fin, on what is a striking
combination of yellow and red.

(Insignia — Plate 2)

65. Great Lakes' Convair CV.580 C-GDTD at Toronto on 18 June 1978.

(Photograph by Russell Brown)

66. Great Northern's Lockheed L.188C Electra N402GN in January 1977.

(Photograph by George Kinney)

67. Gulf-Air's de Havilland Canada DHC-3 Otter C-GLCP in August 1978.

(Photograph by John Kimberley)

68. Haida's de Havilland Canada DHC-2 Beaver C-FGYK in August 1978.

(Photograph by John Kimberley)

69. HARBOR AIRLINES

Harbor Airlines of Oak Harbour, Washington, was formed in March 1971 as Oak Harbor Airlines, and took its current title in May 1974. Today, the airline offers scheduled commuter services within Washington state, to connect Seattle-Tacoma, Oak Harbor and Bellingham. Air-freighting is also undertaken, as is the transportation on Government contract of military personnel between Oak Harbor Air Park and the Naval Air Station on Whidbey Island.

The current fleet consists of 3 Islanders, registered N66HA, N67HA and N69HA.

The Islanders are white overall, with red and blue cheatlines which sweep up through the after part of the tail-fin, and which are repeated on the aircraft engines. Airline titles are bold and clear, running vertically down the tail-fin, and aircraft registrations are similarly large and legible.

(Insignia — Plate 1)

70. HARRISON AIRWAYS

Harrison Airways, based at Vancouver Airport South in British Columbia, was formed in 1960, but went into receivership in 1976. An extensive re-organisation followed, and the airline has made a successful comeback, now operating both passenger and cargo charters in Canada and the USA.

The current fleet consists of 2 ex-Air Canada Viscounts, 2 DC-3s, a CV.440, a Beech 18 and a Cessna 150G.

Although there has been talk for some long time of Harrison Air's taking a new livery, embracing an all-white fuselage encircled by two broad bands, one in red and one in blue, the current standard livery is that illustrated on the CV.440, and worn also by the DC-3s. The upper fuselage is white, and the underside in metal-finish; and a double-cheatline in two tones of blue broadens as it runs aft and sweeps up into the tail-fin. On the CV-440 only, the cheatline is echoed in an underlining of the airline titles; and the colours are repeated on the engines.

(Insignia — Plate 3)

71. HAWAIIAN AIRLINES

Hawaiian Airlines of Honolulu was formed in January 1929 as Inter-Island Airways, to undertake air services in the Hawaiian Islands; at that time, most of the company's stock was owned by the Inter-Island Steam Navigation Co. The airline took its current title in October 1941 and is today a publicly-owned airline, operating scheduled passenger and cargo services between Honolulu (on Oahu island) and the islands of Kauai, Lanai, Molokai, Maui and Hawaii.

Hawaiian Air's current fleet consists of 10 DC-9-50s, 2 DC-9-30s and 2 Electra freighters. More Electras and 3 Shorts 330s are on order.

The livery — by Landor Associates of San Francisco — is one of the most attractive of any US airline. Sweeps of red and magenta streamline the all-white fuselage, drawing the eye to the company symbol on the tail-fin. This symbol combines the classic red hibiscus of Hawaii (the state flower) with the profile of an island girl, wearing a flower in her hair: the girl, appropriately has been named "Pualani" — flower of the sky. Note, too, the highly-distinctive form of airline titling — called a "wordmark" by the airline — on both fuselage and engine; and the smaller version of the flower symbol, for'ard of the fuselage titles.

(Insignia — Plate 3)

72. HOOKER AIR SERVICES

Hooker Air Services of Souix Lookout, Ontario, operates scheduled passenger services, in association with Transair (qv), to link Souix Lookout with Big Trout Lake, Fort Severn, Pickle Lake, Red Lake, Round Lake and Sandy Lake (all in Ontario). On a non-scheduled basis, Hooker serves an even wider area of western Ontario, covering many of the remoter communities between Souix Lookout and Fort Severn (on the shores of Hudson Bay).

Currently, Hooker has a DC-3, 5 Beech 18s, an Otter, a Beaver, a Cessna 185 and a Bellanca 1731AT; a total of 10 aircraft.

The livery consists of a white upper fuselage, with bare-metal underside, wings, engines and tail stabilisters; and a red cheatline (doubled-up for'ard, just aft of the flight-deck windows), with a red and white tail-fin (the two colours separated at the for'ard edge of the rudder). Note that the wing-tips are also in red, that airline titling is in bold block letters, and that the aircraft registration is carried in white on the red section of the fin.

(Insignia — Plate 2)

69. Harbor's Britten-Norman BN-2A Islander N67HA at Bellingham Airport in August 1978.
(Photograph by John Kimberley)

70. Harrison Air's Convair CV.440 CF-HAF in November 1977. (Photograph by John Kimberley)

71. Hawaiian Air's McDonnell Douglas DC-9-51 N619HA "Lehua" in November 1976.
(Photograph from APS files)

72. Hooker Air's Douglas DC-3 C-FGHL departing Winnipeg on 17 June 1978.
(Photograph by F.H. Prior)

73. HUGHES AIRWEST

Hughes Airwest of San Francisco, California, was formed in April 1968 as Air West, following a merger of 3 local-service companies: West Coast Airlines of Seattle; Pacific Air Lines of San Francisco, and Bonanza Air Lines of Phoenix, Arizona. The airline took its current name in April 1970 when the late Howard Hughes gained control through the Hughes Air Corporation (now, the Summa Corporation) and today, operates extensive scheduled services within California and to the states of Washington, Oregon, Montana, Nevada, Utah, Idaho and Arizona. International services reach 6 terminals in Mexico, and 2 in Canada.

The current fleet consists of 5 B.727-200s (plus 2 on order), 26 DC-9-30s (plus 5 on order), 11 DC-9-10s and 5 F-27As.

The livery, with its fuselage in "sundance" yellow, is strikingly attractive; as is the stylised airline titling, which matches the company logo on the tail-fin. Indeed, the yellow colour predominates in Hughes Airwest presentation: the B.727s are termed "sundance flagships", while the airline styles itself as "Top Banana in the West".

(Insignia — Plate 3)

74. ISLAND AIRLINES (CANADA)

Island Airlines of Campbell River, British Columbia, is an operating subsidiary of Haida Airlines; and it may be helpful to the reader to examine both airline entries together. It is of note, however, that — in addition to the scheduled and charter services operated in conjunction with Haida — Island Air is also a fully-certified Cessna dealer, providing sales, maintenance and consulting services.

As a general rule, Island Air's Goose, Islander, Otter and Beavers wear a white livery, with orange cheatline and trim, and with the company logo on the tail-fin. The small Cessnas do not go into a full livery, however, because of the rapid turnover of these aircraft, which would not normally be retained for more than three years. Nonetheless, they do carry either the Haida or Island Air logo, to indicate ownership. It is of note that in Island Air's logo, the black shape on the edge of the orange triangle is a float-plane, in silhouette.

(Insignia — Plate 2)

75.   ISLAND AIRLINES (USA)

Island Airlines of Port Clinton, Ohio, has been in existence since 1929. Billing itself as "the shortest airline in the world", the company operates solely between Port Clinton and the American islands (ie, those south of the Canadian border) in Lake Erie. For all that, the regular scheduled flights are popular with tourists, fishermen and scientists — the last, visiting the glacial grooves at Kelleys Island. The airline maintains its own hotel at Put-In Bay on South Bass Island; and offers charters in addition to its scheduled services.

Island has currently 3 aircraft: a Ford Tri-Motor, an Otter and a Beaver. The Tri-Motor has been out of service for most of 1978, but should be flying again by the end of the year.

The livery consists essentially of an all-white fuselage, with a red cheatline which does not run the length of the aircraft, but starts some way aft of the nose, and ends for'ard of the tail-unit by breaking into three narrower stripes. On the Tri-Motor, the cheatline embraces the cabin-windows; but on the DHC types, runs beneath them. The top of the tail-fin is decorated in dark-blue and red stripes, and horizontal tail stabilisers are tipped in blue (as are the DHC types' wings). In the past, the Tri-Motor has often carried also a blue nose, a blue roof-section above the flight-deck windows and a blue underside to the flat-bottomed fuselage. Note, too, that the red fuselage stripe is repeated on the Tri-Motor's engines.

(Insignia — Plate 1)

76.   KENN BOREK AIR

Kenn Borek Air of Dawson Creek, British Columbia, was formed in May 1966 as Vic Turner Ltd, and took its current name in 1971 when acquired by Borek Construction Ltd. In September 1975, Kenn Borek took over Kenting Aviation (qv) and although both airlines retain their identities, Kenn Borek now conducts Kenting's former DC-3 operations at Resolute. The airline has other bases at Dawson Creek, Frobisher Bay and Inuvik, and flies charter, supply, survey and medical flights into the high Canadian Arctic and Greenland, often in support of oil exploration companies.

Kenn Borek has a fleet of 16 aircraft: 7 DC-3s, 6 Twin Otters, a PA-31 Navajo, a Cessna 172 and a Cessna 150.

Although the airline does operate some aircraft in odd schemes, the standard livery is as illustrated: a red upper fuselage and tail fin, with a black "zig-zagging" cheatline. Note, however, that while the Twin Otter has a white underside, DC-3s in the same scheme have metal-finish undersides, and also a thin white trimline between the cheatline and the red fuselage. The small, scripted form of airline titling is standard to all aircraft.

(Insignia — Plate 4)

73. Hughes Airwest's Boeing 727-2M7 N721RW "Spirit of Gamma" airborne in October 1977.
(Photograph by John Kimberley)

74. Island Air's de Havilland Canada DHC-2 Beaver C-FICK in August 1978.
(Photograph by John Kimberley)

75. Island's Ford 4AT-B Tri-Motor N7584 and de Havilland Canada DHC-2 Beaver N62352 in July
1976.   (Photograph from author's private collection)

76. Kenn Borek's de Havilland Canada DHC-6 Twin Otter C-FABW in January 1977.
                                                          (Photograph by John Kimberley)

77. KENTING AVIATION

Kenting Aviation of Calgary, Alberta, was formed in December 1962 as Atlas
Aviation Ltd, and took its current title ten years later. Now an operating subsidiary
of Kenn Borek Air (qv), Kenting serves the mining and oil industries of the high
Arctic, and several scattered native communities in adjacent areas, providing all the
normal support services and medical charters.

Kenting's current fleet numbers 13 aircraft: 3 Twin Otters, a Canso, 3 Islanders,
2 PA-31 Navajos, a PA-23 Aztec, a PA-18A Super Cub, and 2 Aero Commander 680s.

The smart livery is a derivative of that worn formerly on the DC-3s; and has evolved
as illustrated: an all-white fuselage; twin cheatlines in light and very-dark blue and
the distinctive airline titling, which may be in white and set into the cheatlines (as
shown) or, on some aircraft, in dark-blue against the white of the fuselage. Not all
aircraft wear the "K" symbol on the tail-fin; but many have the cheatline colours
repeated in stripes on the engines, wing-tanks etc. Note, however, that the Twin
Otter has solid dark-blue engines and wing-tips.

(Insignia — Plate 1)

78. KEY AIRLINES

Key Airlines, based at Salt Lake City, Utah, is the state's largest and oldest commuter
airline, and operates scheduled daily passenger and cargo services to the ski and
summer resort of Sun Valley, Idaho, from Salt Lake City and Boise (Idaho). Charter
services are also offered throughout the United States and Canada.

The current fleet consists of 5 CV-440s, an MU-2B-35, a Cessna 414 and 2 PA-31
Navajos; a total of 9 aircraft. It is understood, however, that the Navajos may be
retired shortly.

The small aircraft livery is as illustrated; but the CV.440s wear a more ambitious
scheme: a white upper fuselage and bare-metal underside are divided by two cheatlines (the upper one in brown, and the lower in orange), with a thin white trimline
between. The tail-fin is in orange, and carries the company logo — a stylised white
"K", with an aeroplane shape surmounting it — and airline titling, in brown lower
case letters, is worn in mid-fuselage above the cheatlines. Wings are in bare-metal,
but with brown-painted engines. Just for'ard of the for'ard door, on the white of
the fuselage, is a V-shaped set of brown antlers, with the word "Elkhorn" in brown,
above it; and "at Sun Valley" in orange beneath. Aft of the door is an orange "sun"
symbol, with the words "Sun Valley" in brown beneath.

(Insignia — Plate 3)

79. LAMBAIR

Lambair of Winnipeg, Manitoba, was founded in 1935 as Thomas Lamb Airways, and took its current title in 1969. Today, the airline flies scheduled services linking The Pas, Thompson, Churchill (all in Manitoba) and Rankin Inlet in the Northwest Territories. Extensive passenger and cargo charters are also provided.

The current fleet, consisting both of fixed- and rotary-wing aircraft, comprises 6 DC-3s, a C-46, an F-27F, 3 Twin Otters, 2 Otters, 2 PA-23 Aztecs, an Islander, a Cessna 185, a Cessna 180, 3 Alouettes and a Bell 47G; a total of 22.

Lambair's aircraft wear red and white schemes; but the design thereof differs with individual aircraft. Some have an all-white fuselage and a red cheatline (or twin cheatlines) with the "L" logo in red on a white fin; and others (as illustrated) have an all-red fuselage and a white cheatline, with a white "L" logo on a red fin. The scripted style of airline titling is standard, however, and note that it is always accompanied by the word "Canada". Note also, on the illustrated Twin Otter, the small "polar bear" sticker which indicates that the aircraft has been into the Canadian Arctic (and particularly into the Northwest Territories and Yellowknife).

80. LA RONGE AVIATION SERVICES

La Ronge Aviation Services of La Ronge, Saskatchewan, began operations in 1961, and offers passenger charter services to numerous terminals in northern Canada, including Lynn Lake (Manitoba), and Hay River and Yellowknife (Northwest Territories). Mackenzie Air (qv) is an operating subsidiary of the company.

The fleet consists of 21 aircraft: 5 Twin Otters, 4 Otters, 6 Beavers, 2 PA-23 Aztecs and 4 Cessna 185s.

La Ronge uses two main liveries: that illustrated on the Beaver; and another for its Twin Otters. The "Beaver" livery, as shown, has a white upper fuselage and pale-grey underside, separated by a red cheatline; with the tail-fin similarly divided, having a white upper half and a pale-grey lower half, again separated by a red stripe, which houses the aircraft registration. The "Twin Otter" livery, however, has a red upper fuselage and fin, a thin white cheatline, and dark-blue underside, engines and wing-tips. Note, too, that while most aircraft (and all Twin Otters) have airline titling as shown — ie, "La Ronge" in script form, and the rest in block letters — some do have the whole title in block letters only.

(Insignia — Plate 4)

77. Kenting's de Havilland Canada DHC-6 Twin Otter CF-YLC in May 1977.
(Photograph by John Kimberley)

78. Key's Piper PA-31 Navajo N21KA at Salt Lake City on 26 July 1977.
(Photograph by Ben Knowles, Jr.)

79. Lambair's de Havilland Canada DHC-6 Twin Otter C-FAUS in June 1978.
(Photograph by John Kimberley)

80. La Ronge's de Havilland Canada DHC-2 Beaver C-GMAQ in November 1977.
(Photograph by John Kimberley)

81.   LAS VEGAS AIRLINES

Las Vegas Airlines of Las Vegas, Nevada, was formed in 1973 and is today a charter-tours operator, offering sightseeing and tourist flights to such celebrated places as the Grand Canyon, Hoover Dam, Death Valley and Disneyland. A scheduled service is flown, too, between Las Vegas and Grand Canyon Airport.

The current Las Vegas fleet comprises 5 PA-31 Navajo Chieftains and 3 PA-32 Cherokees (1 leased).

The livery consists of an all-white fuselage, with a curved blue cheatline which sweeps up to fill the for'ard half of the tail-fin. The after half, and the stern of the fuselage, are painted green. Note that the blue cheatline colour is repeated in a stripe on the engine (housing the word "Navajo" in white), that a "Piper" legend is worn in white on the fin, and that the aircraft registration is markedly larger than the neat block-lettered titles carried above the passenger windows.

82.   McCULLY AVIATION

McCully Aviation of Port Alberni, British Columbia, began operations in 1969 with a single Cessna 172 on floats; and now invites one to "come fly with us' from bases at Port Alberni and Tofino (about 60 air miles apart on Vancouver Island's west coast). The majority of the airline's work is on float-equipped aircraft, to service remote coastal fishing and logging areas; and a twice-daily (Monday through Friday) round-trip is flown between Port Alberni and Tofino, serving Green Cove, Bamfield and Ucluelet on the way; and a once-daily round-trip between Tofino and Tahsis, serving Ahousat, Stewardson, Hot Springs Cove, Boat Basin, Hecate Bay and All Way Points. Air ambulance work is also undertaken, as are charter services to the forest industry, sportsmen, campers etc. McCully's fleet consists of 7 aircraft: 3 Beavers, a Cessna 185 and a Cessna 180 (all on floats), a Beech 18 and a Cessna 172 on wheels.

As illustrated, the livery looks extremely smart on the float-Beaver; with an all-white fuselage, a red engine-cowling merging into a red, black-trimmed and tapering cheatline, a parallel red stripe on the tail-fin (housing the aircraft registration, in white), red bands on the white wings, and red tips to both wings and horizontal tail stabilisers. Airline titling is carried in small block letters on the fuselage; and the company's "winged bird" logo is on the upper fin, in red.

(Insignia — Plate 4)

83. MACKENZIE AIR

Mackenzie Air of Edmonton, Alberta, has been an operating subsidiary of La Ronge Aviation Services (qv) since 1975; and today, flies passenger and cargo charter services throughout Alberta, Saskatchewan, Manitoba and the Northwest Territories.

The current fleet consists of 8 aircraft: an FH-227B, a Twin Otter, 2 Beavers, an Islander, a PA-23 Aztec and 2 Learjets. It is of note, however, that La Ronge and Mackenzie Air do exchange aircraft from time to time.

Essentially, the livery consists of an all-white fuselage, a dark-green cheatline trimmed on its underside in red, and the company logo in dark-green on the white fin. A smaller version of the logo — with the colours reversed — appears adjacent to the airline titling. At the time of writing, the FH-227 (C-GMAL), while in a white and green scheme, does not wear the company logo on the fin (nor, incidentally, did its predecessor: F-27F CF-BNX). Another minor peculiarity of recent times is that Beaver C-FGQD wore titles on the port side only; and had red, white-tipped wings.

84. MACKEY INTERNATIONAL AIRLINES

Mackey International Airlines was formed in 1968 to undertake scheduled commuter services from its home base at Fort Lauderdale, Florida, thus succeeding Mackey Airlines Inc, which was absorbed by Eastern Airlines in 1967. Following a route-rationalisation by Eastern, and the demise of Air Caicos and Bahama Airways, Mackey won a number of new routes and expanded operations; and now operates regular services from three Florida terminals (Fort Lauderdale, Miami and West Palm Beach) to destinations in the Bahamas and the British West Indies — "we'll fly you to your place in the sun".

Currently, Mackey has 16 aircraft: 7 DC-6Bs and 9 CV.440s.

The livery consists of an all-white fuselage (but for a metal-finish understrip), with a broad pale-blue, black-trimmed cheatline and the company logo — in pale-blue and black — on the white fin. Airline titles are in standard block capitals, in black. Note that 3 aircraft carry names currently (eg. DC-6B N37580 is "City of Fort Lauderdale"); and that all aircraft have a black anti-dazzle panel on the nose.

(Insignia — Plate 2)

81. Las Vegas' Piper PA-31 Navajo Chieftain N22LV at Grand Canyon Airport on 18 May 1978.
(Photograph by the author)

82. McCully Aviation's de Havilland Canada DHC-2 Beaver C-FGQP in August 1978.
(Photograph by John Kimberley)

83. Mackenzie Air's de Havilland Canada DHC-6 Twin Otter C-FCCE in November 1977.
(Photograph by John Kimberley)

84. Mackey International's Convair CV.440 N442JM in July 1976.
(Photograph from author's private collection)

85. MARCO ISLAND AIRWAYS

Marco Island Airways of Miami, Florida, was founded on 25 September 1972, and is part of the Deltona Corporation. Daily scheduled passenger services are operated between Miami and Marco Island, a Deltona-constructed community on the Gulf of Mexico coast of Florida.

Marco Island is one of the last main operators of the Martin 404, having 4 in full service; and the airline uses also an L.1329 JetStar.

The livery is smart and summery, with an all-white upper fuselage and double cheat-lines in two values of blue. The same two values of blue make up the company logo on the fin, while the darker blue is used on the engines, and for the scripted form of airline titling. Note the square passenger windows, and the black nose and anti-dazzle panel.

(Insignia — Plate 1)

86. MARTIN AIR

Martin Air of Santa Ana, California, uses one PA-31 Navajo Chieftain to operate a twice-daily scheduled passenger service linking Orange County Airport (the airline's main base) with Los Angeles and Calexico, a Californian town on the Mexican border, opposite Mexicali.

The livery consists of an all-white fuselage with a broad orange cheatline which sweeps up into the for'ard half of the tail-fin. In that respect, it is reminiscent of Las Vegas's blue cheatline; but note in this case the stylised "M" which is set into the cheat. The cheatline colour is repeated in a stripe on the engine; and the stand-ard white "Navajo" legend is set into the stripe (again, see Las Vegas' aircraft), with the "Piper" title in white on the orange of the fin. Airline titles are in blue, with the first letter of each word in red; and the aircraft registration is also in red, and in large characters.

(Insignia Plate 2)

87. MIDSTATE AIRLINES

Midstate Airlines of Marshfield, Wisconsin, is the commuter division of Marshfield Airways, which was founded on 17 February 1964. Scheduled daily flights link Chicago (O'Hare) in Illinois with Minneapolis-St. Paul in Minnesota, and with Ashland, Eau Claire, Hayward, Manitowoc, Marshfield, Milwaukee, Sheboygan, Stevens Point, Sturgeon Bay and Wisconsin Rapids, all in Wisconsin. Charter flights are also undertaken.

Midstate's current fleet consists of 3 Metroliners, a Beech 99 and a Beech·18.

The livery is simple, but smart; and suits particularly the long, sleek lines of the Metroliner. The all-white fuselage is offset by a blue cheatline which widens as it runs aft, to sweep up through the tail-fin, and to embrace therein the stylised "M" symbol which is the company's logo. Note that the cheat is underlined by a thin red "straight-through" trimline; and that both cheat and trim colours are repeated on the engines, which are left in an all-metal finish.

(Insignia — Plate 3)

88. MIKSOO AVIATION

Miksoo Aviation of Meadow Lake, Saskatchewan, offers scheduled passengers services throughout western Saskatchewan, linking a number of terminals which include Beauval, Buffalo Narrows, Cluff Lake, Ile-à-la-Crosse, La Loche, Meadow Lake, North Battleford, Saskatoon and Uranium City. Charter services are also operated.

Miksoo's fleet consists of 10 aircraft: a Beech 3NM (Beech 18), 2 PA-31 Navajos, a PA-34 Seneca, a PA-18 Super Cub, 2 Cessna 185s, a Cessna 177, a Cessna 172 and a Cessna 150.

The livery, as illustrated, consists of an all-white fuselage, with a broad blue cheatline, and matching trimline beneath. Cheat and trim stripes are repeated on the engines; and the cheat is "wedged" just aft of the flight-deck windows, to accommodate the black airline titling. Note that, somewhat unusually, the aircraft registration is painted on the tail-fin, rather than the fuselage.

(Insignia — Plate 3)

85. Marco Island's Martin 404 N973M in December 1977.(Photograph from author's private collection)

86. Martin Air's Piper PA-31 Navajo Chieftain N27313 at Santa Ana in May 1978.
(Photograph by John Wegg)

87. Midstate's Swearingen SA226TC Metroliner N162MA at Chicago (O'Hare) in April 1978.
(Photograph by J. Burch)

88. Miksoo's Beech 3NM CF-AID in October 1978.　　　　(Photograph by John Kimberley)

89. MILLARDAIR

Millardair, with its main operations base at Toronto International Airport, Ontario, was known until 1962 as Carl Millard Ltd; and today, undertakes passenger and cargo charter services to various terminals in Canada, the United States and the Caribbean.

The Millardair fleet comprises 3 DC-4s, 9 DC-3s, 4 Beech 18s, a Citation, a PA-31 Navajo Chieftain and 2 PA-30 Twin Comanches; a total of 20 aircraft.

The livery consists essentially of an all-white fuselage, and a complex cheatline in black, red and yellow. These, and the diamond symbol on the engines, are common to the DC-4s and the DC-3s; but some variations appear on the other types of aircraft: the Beech 18s have a multi-cheatline in black and white, with red trimlines above and below; while the Navajo has a triple cheatline in red, black and gold. Many of the DC-3s and DC-4s have names — DC-3 CF-WTU is "The Executive", DC-4 C-GQIA is "Cargoliner I". All aircraft wear a stylised form of Canadian flag, and most carry their registrations in red.

90. MISSISSIPPI VALLEY AIRLINES

Mississippi Valley Airlines was formed on 29 October 1969, and flies extensive commuter services from its home base at La Crosse, Wisconsin, to link with other terminals in Wisconsin, and in Illinois, Iowa, Minnesota and Missouri. In addition, charter services are operated throughout the continental United States.

MVA's current fleet consists of 6 Beech 99s and until the end of 1977, the aircraft wore an all-white scheme with a double-cheatline in two tones of blue. The latest livery, however, puts the aircraft into an all-over cream colour, with twin black cheatlines which house the aircraft registration and the "MVA" logo on nose and tail-fin. But note that the new scheme does not appear to be totally standardised in detail at present: while N487NS (as illustrated) has the tail-fin logo in quite small lettering contained entirely within the twin cheatlines, N247V carries a broad black band — developed out of the cheatlines — across most of the fin, and this in turn carries the logo in much larger and bolder letters. On all aircraft, however, wings and engines remain in a natural-metal finish.

(Insignia — Plate 4)

91.　MUNZ NORTHERN AIRLINES

Munz Northern Airlines of Nome, Alaska, was formed in 1938 as Munz Airways, and took its present name in 1962. Today, the airline operates regular passenger, cargo and mail services to link Nome with some 25 communities on the Seward Peninsula, St. Lawrence Island and Diomede Island, all in western Alaska. Since delivery in June 1977 of the airline's Islanders, further services have been undertaken, based at Kotzebue on the Baldwin Peninsula.

The current fleet consists of 7 Islanders, 3 Aero Commander 680s, a Dornier Do28 and a Cessna 205.

The livery is a striking combination of orange, white and black; with an orange upper fuselage, a white underside and a black orange-trimmed cheatline. All three colours are repeated on the engines and the tail-fin, while the main undercarriage struts are in black, and the wings are white. Note that the company logo is worn on the fuselage and that, in the airline titling, the word "Munz" is in script form and the rest in block capitals.

(Insignia — Plate 3)

92.　NATIONAL AIRLINES

National Airlines of Miami began scheduled services on 15 October 1934. Since that time, the airline has grown to become one of the leading operators in the USA; with routes from Miami to New York and Boston in the north, to Los Angeles and San Francisco in the west, and numerous terminals between. On 15 June 1970, National became the third scheduled US carrier across the North Atlantic, with a daily round-trip between Miami and London; with Paris added in 1977, and Frankfurt and Amsterdam from 1978.

National's fleets consists solely of DC-10s and B.727s, having 4 DC-10-30s, 11 DC-10-10s, 24 B.727-200s and 13 B.727-100s; a total of 52 aircraft.

The bright "sunshine" livery of orange and yellow, designed by Gene Moore of Tiffany Inc., was adopted in December 1967 and first appeared on DC-8 N6572C. National's "Fly Me" marketing campaign, introduced in 1972, led to all aircraft being accorded a girl's name, carried in large colour splashes aft of the flight deck windows; and January 1977 saw yet another dimension to the "name game" when some DC-10s took the names of famous showbiz personalities, carried in the same place as the old colour splash, but in the form of the personality's autograph, with a cartoon outline of his head. Shortly thereafter, however, National abolished aircraft names; and at the same time, fuselages went from white upper surfaces and metal underside, to an all-white finish.

(Insignia — Plate 3)

89. Millardair's Douglas DC-4 C-GQIB "The Skytrader" at Toronto on 16 June 1978.
(Photograph by Russell Brown)

90. Mississippi Valley's Beech 99 N847NS at Chicago (O'Hare) in April 1978. (Photograph by J. Burch)

91.   Munz Northern's Britten-Norman BN-2A Islander N35MN "Kiana" in June 1977.
(Photograph from author's private collection)

92.   National's McDonnell Douglas DC-10-30 N81NA at London Heathrow in January 1978.
(Photograph by A.J. Kemsley)

93. NEVADA AIRLINES

Nevada Airlines of Las Vegas, Nevada, began scheduled passenger services on 1 January 1974; and operates regular flights — from Las Vegas to Grand Canyon Airport — which can include a sight-seeing route over the canyon, a bus-tour and lunch. The airline offers also charter services "to any place, any time."

The Nevada fleet consists of 3 DC-3s and 2 Beechcraft Tradewinds, the latter being a tri-gear conversion of the Beech C45.

The livery is essentially a combination of white, red and yellow; and the Tradewinds scheme is as illustrated. The three DC-3s operate, however, in slightly differing schemes: DC-3 N138D wears a red and yellow "straight-through" double-cheatline, and red and yellow horizontal half-stripes on the for'ard part of the tail-fin; N139D has the same cheatline, but has diagonal stripes in red and yellow running completely across the tail-fin; and N163E has a much broader double-cheatline in orange and mustard, which sweeps up through the tail-fin, with engine cowling-tops in orange, and broad wing stripes — running aft from the engines — in mustard.

(Insignia — Plate 1)

94. NEW YORK AIRWAYS

New York Airways was formed in August 1949 to undertake scheduled helicopter services in the New York area. Mail services began in October 1952 between the three main New York airports — Newark, La Guardia and Idlewild/Kennedy — and passenger services over the same routes started in July 1953. Today, the airline links all three airports with Morristown (New Jersey) and the Wall Street Heliport; and may shortly operate also from the Manhattan World Trade Center.

In March 1970, the airline re-equipped with S-61Ls (replacing Boeing-Vertol 107s), each aircraft having 30 seats. This brought about an operation now known as the "30-30 service": 30 seats available every 30 minutes from each of the three airports; which is currently achieved with 3 S-61Ls, registered N617PA, N618PA and N620PA.

The livery consists of an all-white fuselage, with blue and black engine housing. The main airline titling is worn in mid-fuselage, in red, and the red and white company logo is on the tail. Note that both logo and titling appear also, together and in much smaller form, on the nose of the aircraft; as does the registration.

(Insignia — Plate 3)

95. NORCANAIR

Norcanair (North Canada Air Ltd) of Prince Albert, Saskatchewan, was formed in August 1947 as Saskatchewan Government Airways (Saskair) and became a privately-owned company, in the current name, in March 1965. Today, the airline operates scheduled passenger and cargo services from Prince Albert to Buffalo Narrows, Fond du Lac, Lac La Ronge, Regina, Saskatoon, Stony Rapids and Uranium City (all in Saskatchewan). Group charters, water-bombing and heavy freighting are also under-taken.

Norcanair's fleet consists of 31 aircraft: 5 F-27As, 3 DC-3s, 4 Cansos, a Bristol 170, 3 Otters, 6 Beavers, 4 PA-23 Aztecs and 5 Cessna 185s.

The livery consists essentially of an all-white fuselage, with dark-blue cheatline and red trim; but variations occur on certain types of aircraft. The Aztecs have a main cheatline in bright red, trimmed in black, with the colours repeated on the engines, and on the leading and upper edges of the fin. The Cessnas have thin red and black cheatlines which broaden and zig-zag as they run aft. The Cansos do not generally wear airline titling, but have an all-silver fuselage and a white tail, with orange dayglo fuselage bands, engine cowlings, wing leading-edges and tips, fin-top and fleet number. Most, but not all, aircraft carry the company's "compass" logo on the tail-fin.

(Insignia — Plate 1)

96. NORDAIR

Nordair, based at Montreal International Airport, Quebec, was formed in 1957 by the merger of Mont Laurier Aviation and Boreal Airways; and today, operates an extensive network of scheduled passenger and cargo services in Quebec and Ontario, and to the Arctic regions, where services are centred also on Frobisher Bay (North-west Territories). Inclusive-tours, ad-hoc charters and ice-reconnaissance (under Government contract) are also undertaken.

The Nordair fleet comprises 6 B.737-200s, 3 FH-227s, a DC-8-61CF and an L.188C Electra; a total of 11 aircraft.

The livery is smart, but simple; consisting of a white upper fuselage and light-grey underside, with a broad blue cheatline and matching tail-fin. The large white "N" logo on the tail contrasts with the small, black airline titles, in slightly-slanted block letters. Note also the black nose-tip and anti-dazzle panel.

It is understood that a proposed take-over by Air Canada will leave Nordair as an operating subsidiary and that, thus, the livery will survive for the foreseeable future.

(Insignia — Plate 1)

93.   Nevada's Beechcraft Tradewinds N481E at Grand Canyon Airport on 18 May 1978.
(Photograph by the author)

94.   New York's Sikorsky S-61Ls N617PA and N618PA in October 1975. (Photograph from APS files)

95.   Norcanair's de Havilland Canada DHC-3 Otter C-FJFJ in November 1977.
(Photograph by John Kimberley)

96.   Nordair's Boeing 737-242C CF-NAH at Toronto on 11 June 1978.   (Photograph by Russell Brown)

97. NORTH CENTRAL AIRLINES

North Central Airlines of Minneapolis, Minnesota, was formed on 15 May 1944 as Wisconsin Central Airlines and in that name, began scheduled services on 24 February 1948. In 1952, the airline moved from Wisconsin to Minneapolis, and changed its name to North Central. Today, the airline serves some 90 cities in 14 states, with international services to Toronto and Winnipeg in Canada. Charter services — both domestic and international — are also offered.

North Central's fleet consists of 57 aircraft: 12 DC-9-50s (plus 3 on order), 19 DC-9-30s and 26 CV.580s.

The livery consists of a white upper fuselage and metal underside, with a broad light-blue cheatline and dark-blue trim. Airline titling is also in the darker blue, as is the highlight of the scheme: the mallard duck logo. Set against a circle which represents the sun by day and the moon by night, and now carried on aircraft tail-fins, the duck was incorporated into the cheatline on Wisconsin Central aircraft and has thus been the company's insignia in both past and present guises. Note that the duck always "flies" forward.

(Insignia — Plate 2)

98. NORTHWARD AIRLINES

Northward Airlines, with its headquarters at St. Albert, Alberta, was formed in 1965; and today, offers scheduled passenger services to 25 communities in the Northwest Territories and the Yukon, from bases at Whitehorse (Yukon) and Inuvik, Yellowknife, Cambridge Bay and Norman Wells (all in NWT). Charter services are also undertaken.

The fleet consists of 5 aircraft: 3 Twin Otters, an F-27 and a Beech 99.

The livery embraces an all-white fuselage, with a broad cheatline in bright red and black block-lettered airline titles. The company logo, a white "N" within a black oval adorns the tail-fin; and, on the Beech 99, the engines are in white. Only very minor variations occur on the other types: eg, the F-27 has bare-metal engines and a thin bare-metal understrip to the fuselage.

(Insignia — Plate 1)

99. NORTHWEST ORIENT AIRLINES

Northwest Airlines Inc. of Minneapolis-St. Paul, Minnesota, was formed in 1926 as
Northwest Airways and adopted its current corporate title in 1934, taking over
Northern Air Transport in the same year. The name "Northwest Orient Airlines" is
an operating title, the airline having flown Far East services since 1947. Today,
Northwest's route-map spans the continental United States, and to Hawaii, Alaska
and Canada; and extends across the Pacific to Korea, Japan, Okinawa, Taiwan, the
Philippines and Hong Kong. Transatlantic services to six European countries
(including Scotland) have CAB approval, but have yet to start.

Northwest's fleet comprises 5 B.747-200s, 12 B.747-100s, 4 B.747Fs, 22 DC-10-40s,
40 B.727-200s, 25 B.727-100s and 2 B.707-351s; a total of 110 aircraft.

The livery is distinctive; with silver roof and fuselage underside, a broad white band
between and a dark-blue fore-shortened cheatline. Tail-fin and airline titling are in
red, with the company logo (also in red) aft of the titling on either side of the fuselage. The B.747Fs, however, while retaining the red tail, are otherwise in an all-over
metal finish, and carry the red titling "Northwest Orient Cargo" without the company logo.   (Insignia — Plate 1)

100. NORTHWEST TERRITORIAL AIRWAYS

Northwest Territorial Airways (NWT Air) of Yellowknife, Northwest Territories,
began operations in 1962; and in 1975, acquired the licences of International Jet
Air of Calgary. Today, the airline flies scheduled passenger services from Yellowknife,
Calgary and Edmonton to Port Radium, Coppermine, Lady Franklin Point and
Cambridge Bay. Charter services are also operated in support of the mining, oil and
gas industries in Northern Canada.

The NWT Air fleet numbers 7 aircraft: 4 DC-3s, 2 DC-6s and an Electra.

The latest livery can be taken to be that on the Electra (as illustrated), which was
repainted in 1978 from its old International Jet Air scheme, but in fact only minor
differences exist in the variations on the other types: the DC-3s have merely the
word "Northwest" as fuselage titling; while the DC-6s have "Northwest Territorial
Airways" above the cheatline and "NWT Air" in black beneath the cheatline for'ard.
Standard to all types, however, is the basic scheme of white upper fuselage, silver
underside, and red cheatline and tail, with white "NWT Air" titles on the fin.
                                                                       (Insignia — Plate 4)

97.   North Central's McDonnell Douglas DC-9-31 N965N at Toronto on 21 May 1978.
(Photograph by Russell Brown)

98.   Northward's Beech 99 C-GXFC in October 1978.   (Photograph by John Kimberley)

99. Northwest Orient's McDonnell Douglas DC-10-40 N155US in April 1976.

(Photograph from author's private collection)

100. Northwest Territorial's Lockheed L.188A Electra CF-IJV in September 1978.

(Photograph by John Kimberley)

101. OKANAGAN HELICOPTERS

Okanagan Helicopters, based at Vancouver International Airport, British Columbia, was formed in 1947; and is today the largest helicopter operator in Canada, and engaged in every aspect of helicopter activity: forestry, mining, oil and gas exploration, surveying, construction, agriculture, rescue, patrol and salvage operations. A mountain-flying helicopter training school is also operated. Subsidiary companies are Canadian Helicopters and Lac St. Jean Aviation (both in Montreal), Universal Helicopters (Ottawa), Dominion-Pegasus Helicopters (Toronto), Sept-Iles Helicopter Services (Sept-Isles) and Associated Helicopters (Edmonton).

The fleet comprises 97 JetRangers, 8 Alouettes, 7 S-61s, 3 S-58s, an S-55, 5 Bell 205As and 7 Bell 212s; a total of 128 aircraft.

Although the livery varies slightly between different types of helicopter, all aircraft are predominantly orange, with white cheatlines, bands or tails. As a general rule, the black, block-lettered airline titling appears towards the tail of an aircraft, on a white stripe, while aircraft registrations are usually placed for'ard, on the nose.

(Insignia — Plate 3)

102. OZARK AIR LINES

Ozark Air Lines of St. Louis, Missouri, began scheduled services on 26 September 1950, using DC-3s between St. Louis and Chicago. Today, however, the airline serves some 58 cities over an unduplicated route-mileage of 8,400 miles; with a network spreading over some two-thirds of the United States — from Minneapolis-St. Paul in the north to Dallas in the south, and from Denver in the Rocky Mountains to New York.

Ozark's first jet, a DC-9, was delivered in May 1966; and the same year saw the introduction of its other current aircraft, the FH-227B. At present Ozark has 19 FH-227s and 32 DC-9s, a total of 51 aircraft.

The name "Ozark" is said to derive from the French "bois aux arc" (wood of bows) and the airline shares the name today with an area of highlands stretching over Missouri, Arkansas, Oklahoma, Kansas and Illinois. Highlight of the smart green and white livery is the stylised interpretation of three swallows. This logo has romantic connotations: swallows are traditionally symbols of safe travel and good luck; while the birds themselves are noted for their scheduled flights (eg, the famous arrival and departure at the Mission of San Juan Capistrano, on the same days every year since the mission was built in 1806). Certainly, Ozark's swallows are an effective addition to the livery; note that they "fly" forwards on both sides of the tail-fin.

(Insignia — Plate 3)

103. PACIFIC ALASKA AIRLINES

Pacific Alaska Airlines of Fairbanks, Alaska, was known formerly as Aero Retardant Inc., and was formed in 1972 by the airline's current chairman, Mr. Don Gilbertson. In 1973, Pacific Alaska bought Pan Alaska Airways, a Fairbanks-based air taxi operation; and today, the airline operates commercial passenger and cargo charter services, principally within Alaska.

The fleet numbers 6 aircraft: 3 DC-6s, 2 F-27s and a PA-31 Navajo.

The livery, as illustrated, consists of an all-white fuselage, with a double-cheatline in red and black, broadening from the nose to form a long arrow-shape across the length of the aircraft. This arrow-theme is repeated on the tail-fin, and both airline titling and aircraft registration are in red. Note, however, that the DC-6s wear a rather different scheme; with a white upper fuselage, silver underside, a narrow regular double-cheatline in reddish-gold and black, and bright red wing-tips and tail-fin band.

(Insignia — Plate 3)

104. PACIFIC COASTAL AIRLINES

Pacific Coastal Airlines of Cassidy, British Columbia, was formed in 1956 as Cassidair Services, and took its present title in 1965. Thrice-daily passenger services connect Qualicum and Port Alberni with Vancouver, and extensive charter and air-taxi operations are also flown. The airline is associated additionally with McGillivary Helicopters Ltd.

Pacific Coastal's current fleet consists of 2 DC-3s, 3 PA-28 Cherokees, a PA-23 Apache, a PA-31 Navajo, an Islander, a Beech 18 and 2 Cessna 172s; a total of 11 aircraft.

The livery illustrated on DC-3 CF-PWI is perhaps the most attractive of those used by Pacific Coastal; and is currently the only one which uses the tail-fin "gull" logo. It is, however, quite different to that worn by the other DC-3 (C-FKAZ) which has a white upper fuselage and tail-fin, a silver underside, a blue, yellow-trimmed cheatline and no logo. The Apache and the Islander, on the other hand, have all-white fuselages and green and black cheatlines; although, again, the schemes differ in detail. All aircraft, however, use the form of airline titling illustrated; with "Pacific Coastal" in block letters, and "Airlines" in script.

101. Okanagan's Sikorsky S-61L C-FOKB in June 1978.   (Photograph from APS files)

102. Ozark's McDonnell Douglas DC-9-15 N971Z in August 1976.

(Photograph from author's private collection)

103. Pacific Alaska's Fairchild F-27J N777DG in August 1978.   (Photograph by John Kimberley)

104. Pacific Coastal's Douglas DC-3 CF-PWI in August 1978.   (Photograph by John Kimberley)

105. PACIFIC SOUTHWEST AIRLINES

Pacific Southwest Airlines (PSA) of San Diego, California, began life with one leased DC-3 in 1949 and has expanded to become a major force in Californian aviation, with high-frequency, low-fare intra-state services linking San Diego, Long Beach, Ontario, Los Angeles, Hollywood/Burbank, Fresno, San Jose, San Francisco, Oakland, Stockton, Lake Tahoe and Sacramento. In addition, PSA has interests in such things as hotels and broadcasting, and maintains a flying school for conversion to the smaller Boeing jets.

Currently, PSA has 34 aircraft: 24 B.727-200s, 6 B.727-100s and 4 Electras.

The highlight of PSA's livery is undoubtedly the "smiling face" on all its aircraft — but the colours, too, are eyecatching and imaginative. Until mid-1977, the cheatlines and "rooster tails" were in fuschia, orange and red; but have gone now to orange, red-orange and dark-red, because — it is said — the fuschia colour faded too quickly in the Californian sun. A more recent change is that airline titling has gone from solid-black letters to the white, black-outlined type, as illustrated.

(Insignia — Plate 1)

106. PACIFIC WESTERN AIRLINES

Pacific Western Airlines, based at Vancouver International Airport, British Columbia, was founded on 1 July 1945 as Central British Columbia Airways, and took it current name on 15 May 1953. The airline absorbed BC Air Lines in 1970; and to-day operates extensive scheduled and non-scheduled services throughout British Columbia, Alberta and the Northwest Territories, and to Seattle in Washington state. Worldwide passenger and cargo services are also offered. PWA has applied to take over Transair (qv); but it is likely that both airlines will retain their current identities post-merger.

PWA's current fleet numbers 20 aircraft: 12 B.737-200s, a B.727-100, 2 B.707s, 3 Hercules, a DC-3 and a CV.640.

The livery consists of a white upper fuselage and silver underside, with a dark-blue cheatline which broadens as it runs aft, and sweeps up to embrace the greater part of the tail-fin. The company logo, on the fin, is in red and light-blue, and airline titling — in a stylised form of block-lettering — is in red. Note also the Canadian flag, worn unusually far for'ard, beneath the flight-deck windows.

(Insignia — Plate 3)

107. PAN AMERICAN WORLD AIRWAYS

Pan American World Airways was established in 1927 as a mail carrier between Key West, Florida and Havana; and has grown from the humble operator of 3 Fokker trimotors to become one of the world's foremost airlines, with a vast global route pattern. In addition, Pan Am operates limited services within the USA, and a system of local services in Germany.

Pan Am's current fleet comprises 28 B.747-100s, a B.747-200, 5 B.747Fs, 6 B.747SPs, (plus 4 on order), 46 B.707-320s and 13 B.727-100s; a total of 99 aircraft. 12 L-1011-500s are also on order.

Pan Am's basic livery has been unchanged for many years, but the airline titling on the fuselage has borne a number of modifications: through the full title of "Pan American" (introduced with the B.707) to the contracted name of "Pan Am" on introduction of the B.747 in December 1969. Latest modifications heralded the introduction of the B.747SP in early 1976 when the sizes of the Pan Am titling and the tail-fin disc (a globe to symbolise the world-wide nature of Pan Am's operations) were increased, the Stars and Stripes was sloped at the top of the fin and a more flowing script adopted for the aircrafts' "Clipper" names. Note that the B.747 freighters carry the word "Cargo" in black after the Pan Am titling on the fuselage, and beneath the disc on the fin.

(Insignia — Plate 1)

108. PANARCTIC OILS

Panarctic Oils, with its head Office at Calgary, Alberta, was incorporated in 1966 as an oil and gas exploration company, and began its drilling programme in 1968. In the same year, the company purchased its first Twin Otter; and today, uses two Twin Otters — stationed in Rea Point on Melville Island, the main base camp — to transport men and equipment between the base camp and the various drilling sites. As Panarctic operates solely in the Arctic Islands, these aircraft are equipped with flotation tyres which enable summer operation on soft airstrips, and landing on snow.

Panarctic's current Twin Otters are registered C-GPAO and C-GXXB; and Twin Otter enthusiasts will be interested to note that their recently-retired CF-PAT (illustrated here) is a Series 100 and c/n 2. (C/n 1 is retained by DHC).

The livery is one of smart simplicity; with an all-white fuselage and twin cheatlines in blue and red. The engines, painted black, are trimmed in white and red; and the company logo — a white stylised maple-leaf and neat white titling within a blue circle — is worn on the tail-fin.

(Insignia — Plate 1)

105. PSA's Lockheed L.188A Electra N6106A at San Francisco on 25 May 1978.
(Photograph by the author)

106. Pacific Western's Boeing 737-275 C-FPWW in April 1978.   (Photograph by John Kimberley)

107. Pan Am's Boeing 747SP-21 N536PA "Clipper Lindbergh" at San Francisco on 12 May 1978.
(Photograph by the author)

108. Panarctic's de Havilland Canada DHC-6 Twin Otter CF-PAT in August 1977.
(Photograph by John Kimberley)

109. PEACE AIR

Peace Air of Peace River, Alberta, began operations in 1962 as Peace River Air Services, and took its present name in 1968. Today, bases are maintained at High Level, Fort Vermilion, Slave Lake and High Prairie (all in Alberta) and the airline offers charter, sales, repair and rental services. A Government-approved flying-school is also operated.

Peace Air has currently 23 aircraft: a PA-31 Navajo, a PA-23 Aztec, an Islander, a Cessna 402B, 11 Cessna 185s, 2 Cessna 180s, a Cessna 172 and 5 Cessna 150s.

The Cessna 185 livery can be taken as standard, because Peace Air has so many of them; and this, as illustrated, consists of an all-white fuselage with red cheatline, trim, wing-tips and fin-top. Variations do occur on other types, however: eg, the Cessna 402 has an all-white fuselage, but brown and tan cheatlines and trim; and the Islander's all-white fuselage has double-cheatlines in two values of green. Most aircraft wear the airline titling within an oval, as illustrated; but the Islander has dark-green block-lettering on the fuselage.

110. PEM-AIR

Pem-Air of Pembroke, Ontario, commenced services on 7 May 1970, using Beech 18s, when it inherited the Pembroke-Toronto route from Royalair, on that company's liquidation. Today, Pem-Air holds additionally licences for domestic and international charters.

Pem-Air has currently five aircraft: 4 DC-3s and a PA-31 Navajo.

The Navajo livery, as illustrated, consists of a white upper fuselage and yellow under-side, with a narrow blue cheatline repeated on the engines, and on the tail-fin to enclose a section in yellow. Note, however, that the DC-3s wear currently a different livery; having an all-white fuselage with a blue, red-trimmed cheatline and blue engine cowlings. The airline titling, in white on the cheatline, has as its leading letter a stylised, winged "P".

(Insignia — Plate 2)

111. PIEDMONT AIRLINES

Piedmont Airlines of Winston-Salem, North Carolina, was incorporated as Piedmont Aviation on 2 July 1940, as an aircraft sales and service operation. The company maintained this role during and after World War II; until, on 1 January 1948, the Airline Division was formed and Piedmont Airlines began scheduled operations on 20 February 1948. Today, Piedmont serves some 80 cities in 12 eastern states and the District of Columbia; ranging from Memphis, Tennessee to New York, and from Chicago to Charleston, South Carolina, on a route-network of more than 11,000 miles.

The current Piedmont fleet numbers 49 aircraft: 23 YS-11As, 23 B.737-200s and 3 B.727-100s.

The livery consists of a white upper fuselage and silver underside, with a broad "straight-through" cheatline in blue. The company's "winged bird" motif is also in blue, on the tail-fin, with airline titling in red beneath. Main airline titles, also in red but much larger, are worn conventionally on the upper fuselage. Note that most aircraft are called "Pacemakers"; eg, the first YS-11 aircraft (delivered May 1968) was named "Cherry Blossom Pacemaker" in recognition of its Japanese origin. Another first was "Yadkin Valley Pacemaker" (N753N), illustrated here and the first aircraft to wear the current livery, on 15 June 1974.

(Insignia — Plate 4)

112. PRECISION VALLEY AVIATION

Precision Valley Aviation of North Springfield, Vermont operates scheduled passenger commuter services to link Springfield with Rutland and Burlington (also in Vermont), Boston (Massachusetts) and Manchester and Keene (New Hampshire). Some scheduled cargo flights are also operated, and cargo charters are available; and the airline is a scheduled mail-carrier under contract to the US Post Office.

Precision's current fleet numbers 11 aircraft: 2 PA-31 Navajo Chieftains, 2 PA-32 Cherokees, 5 Beech 18s, a Cessna 195 and a Waco UPF-7.

The livery, as illustrated, consists of an all-white fuselage with the usual Chieftain double-cheatline, this time in red and a greenish-brown. The latter colour is used for the "P" symbol on the after fuselage; and both colours are repeated on the engines. Note that airline titling is in the form "Precision Commuter"; with the word "Precision" in attractive script, and "Commuter" in smaller block letters.

(Insignia — Plate 2)

109. Peace Air's Cessna A185F C-GDYS in May 1977.   (Photograph by John Kimberley)

110. Pem-Air's Piper PA-31 Navajo CF-GFJ in August 1978.   (Photograph by John Kimberley)

111. Piedmont's Boeing 737-2H5 N753N "Yadkin Valley Pacemaker" in September 1976.
(Photograph from APS files)

112. Precision's Piper PA-31 Navajo Chieftain N27205 in July 1977. (Photograph by Bruce Johnson)

113. PRINAIR

Prinair (Puerto Rico International Airlines) is based at San Juan International Airport, Puerto Rico, and was founded on 4 July 1964, as Ponce Air. Today, Prinair operates extensive high-frequency commuter services to link San Juan with ten other terminals in Puerto Rico, and with points in the US and British Virgin Islands, the Leeward Islands, the Netherlands Antilles, Guadeloupe and the Dominican Republic.

Prinair owns the world's largest fleet of Heron aircraft, having twenty-nine, all Riley Herons re-engined with Lycomings.

The livery is essentially standard to all aircraft; having an all-white fuselage and a broad cheatline which sweeps up to embrace most of the tail-fin and to encompass thereon the company's "heron" logo, usually in red. The colour of the cheatline, however, varies from aircraft to aircraft; and may be beige, red, grey, green, black, brown, orange, blue, bronze or yellow. Note, too, the stylised form of the black airline titling, and the fact that aircraft registrations are always in white, on the cheatline.

(Insignia — Plate 3)

114. PROVINCETOWN-BOSTON AIRLINE

The Provincetown-Boston Airline (PBA) of Provincetown, Massachusetts, began operations in 1949 and flies scheduled commuter services between Provincetown (on Cape Cod) and Boston's Logan International Airport (hence, the airline's name). In addition, PBA offers charter services throughout the United States and runs air-taxi services between Provincetown, Boston and Chatham (Mass.). Naples Airlines of Naples, Florida, is a division of PBA. Formed in 1960 to utilise PBA's aircraft and crews in off-peak periods, Naples now flies regular services between its base and Miami and Tampa, with 3 daily round-trip flights to each destination.

The combined PBA/Naples fleet numbers 26 aircraft: 9 DC-3As, 7 Martin 404s, 3 PA-23 Aztecs, a PA-23 Apache, a PA-32 Cherokee, 2 Cessna 402Bs, an Islander, a Stinson SM8A and a Piper J3C-65.

The livery consists of an all-white fuselage, with a red, dark-blue trimmed cheatline, red and dark-blue fin stripes and the company logo, which is a white bird surmounting a red "PBA" motif and set in a dark-blue circle. Until relatively recently, Naples' aircraft have carried their own titles, while retaining the PBA fin logo; but all aircraft seem more generally now to have a common title as illustrated. Note that Naples uses "Airlines", in the plural form, while PBA uses the singular "Airline".

(Insignia — Plate 1)

115. PTARMIGAN AIRWAYS

Ptarmigan Airways of Yellowknife, Northwest Territories, was formed in 1961, and operates passenger and cargo services from Yellowknife to Snowdrift, Fort Reliance, Rae-Edzo, Lac La Martre and Rae Lakes (all in NWT). Charter and other non-scheduled flights are also undertaken.

Ptarmigan's fleet comprises a Twin Otter, 2 Turbo Beavers, a Beaver, a PA-31 Navajo, a PA-23 Aztec and 5 Cessna 185s; a total of 11 aircraft.

The livery is striking; with an all-yellow fuselage, tail and wings, offset by a black, tapering cheatline. The upper halves of the engines are also in black, as are the tips of the horizontal tail-stabilisers and the anti-dazzle panel on the nose. Note the "winged" letter "P" in the stylised airline titles, and the fact that the words "Yellowknife NWT" are carried in very small lettering beneath.

(Insignia — Plate 3)

116. QUEBECAIR

Quebecair, based at Montreal International Airport, Quebec, was formed in 1946 as Rimouski Aviation Syndicate, became Rimouski Airlines in 1947, and merged in 1953 with the Gulf Aviation Company to become Quebecair. Today, scheduled passenger and cargo services link Montreal and Quebec City with more than 45 terminals in Quebec and Labrador; and charter and inclusive-tour flights reach Hawaii, Mexico, the Bahamas, the Caribbean, Europe and North Africa.

Quebecair's current fleet numbers 15 aircraft: 2 B.707-120Bs, a B.727-100, 4 F.27s, 3 BAC-111s and 5 CV.580s.

The livery consists of a white upper fuselage and silver underside; with two narrow cheatlines in blue, passing above and below the passenger-windows. The lower cheatline goes "straight-through"; but the upper one broadens as it turns up across the tail-fin, and embraces thereon the stylised "Q" logo, in which the "tail" of the "Q" is a bird. Airline titling is also in blue.

(Insignia — Plate 4)

113. Prinair's de Havilland DH.114 Riley Herons N576PR, N575PR and N4789C in March 1976.
(Photograph from APS files)

114. PBA's Douglas DC-3A N137PB in April 1978. (Photograph by IAPS, J. Plaisier)

115. Ptarmigan's de Havilland Canada DHC-6 Twin Otter C-GARW in June 1978.
(Photograph by John Kimberley)

116. Quebecair's Boeing 707-123B C-GQBH at Toronto in June 1978. (Photograph by John Kimberley)

117. RANSOME AIRLINES

Ransome Airlines, with its headquarters at North Philadelphia Airport, Pennsylvania, began operations on 2 March 1967, and flies as part of the Allegheny Commuter system, created to offer frequent services, over relatively-short routes, in areas not served by the major carriers; thereby giving passengers the convenience of easy connections with main hub terminals. Ransome achieves this by feeding passengers from its home base, from Trenton and Newark (both in New Jersey) and from New London/Groton (Connecticut) into Philadelphia International and Washington National Airports.

Ransome's current fleet numbers 10 aircraft: 9 Nord 262As and a Twin Otter; and it is of note that the interiors of the 262s were completely redesigned and retrofitted by the airline. Two Dash 7s are on order, for 1979 delivery.

The livery is that introduced in early 1977, and common to all Allegheny Commuter aircraft; and was designed by Landor Associates of San Francisco. This new design is distinguished by the stylised "A" in two values of red, carried on the tail-fin (and, by some airlines, on the fuselage, too) and is offset by a red cheatline trimmed in gold. The cheatline relates, of course, to the similar stripe on Allegheny's jets, and lends compatibility to the design schemes for the total Allegheny system, while nonetheless giving the individual elements imaginative and eye-catching identities.

(Insignia — Plate 3)

118. RICH INTERNATIONAL AIRWAYS

Rich International Airways of Miami, Florida, started operations in January 1971; and in July 1976, was designated a US supplemental carrier licensed to fly all-cargo services from terminals in the states of Florida and Georgia to Canada, Mexico, the Caribbean and Central America. Charter services from Miami to the Bahamas and Turks and Caicos are also offered.

Rich has a current fleet of 5 aircraft: 2 DC-6s and 3 C-46s.

The C-46 livery, as illustrated, consists of a white upper fuselage and silver underside, with a dark-blue cheatline and a dark-blue tail-fin, on which is worn the large white "R" logo. Note also, on the C-46s, the repetition of the aircraft registration, being both on after-fuselage and nose. The DC-6s offer a slight variation to the scheme in that they have a main cheatline in light-blue, underlined by a dark-blue trimline.

(Insignia — Plate 4)

119. RIO AIRWAYS

Rio Airways, based at Killeen Municipal Airport, Texas, can best trace its origins through the actions of its chairman, Ted C. Connell. Connell began with DAL Airlines and in 1967, obtained Hood Airlines and merged the two operations under the Hood Airlines name. In 1971, Hood purchased Rio Airways and retained the Rio name in the new merger. Today, Rio serves Dallas-Fort Worth Regional Airport, Wichita Falls/Sheppard Air Force Base, Temple and Waco; and is the US' sixth largest commuter airline. Substantial charter work is also undertaken in the USA, Canada and Mexico.

Rio's current fleet numbers 11 aircraft: 6 Beech 99s and 5 Twin Otters.

The Beech 99 livery, designed by the Southwest Advertising Company of Waco, Texas, consists of an all-white fuselage, with tail-fin, twin cheatlines and engine-stripes in a single colour (which varies between aircraft — N17RA is yellow). An arrow symbol is worn on the tail-fin and airline titling, in block letters, breaks the twin cheatlines on the after-fuselage. The Twin Otters, on the other hand, have taken a new livery, as illustrated; having an all-cream fuselage, with a triple cheatline in orange, white and red, and the company's "colour splash" logo set boldly into mid-fuselage. Note also the black engine-tops and anti-dazzle panel.

(Insignia — Plate 2)

120. ROCKY MOUNTAIN AIRWAYS

Rocky Mountain Airways of Denver, Colorado, was formed in 1964 as Vail Airways; and operates scheduled intra-state passenger services to link Denver with the ski-resorts of Aspen, Steamboat Springs, Vail/Eagle and Winter Park/Granby; and with Craig and Leadville (the highest airport in the USA).

Rocky Mountain's current fleet numbers 8 aircraft: 4 Twin Otters, 2 Beech 65 King Airs, an Aero Commander 500 and a Dash-7 (with two more on order).

The livery consists of an all-white fuselage, with a dark-blue, red-trimmed cheatline. Cheat and trim colours are repeated on the engines, and airline titling is carried beneath the cheatline, for'ard. Note particularly the clever arrangement of the "RMA" logo on the fin, so set that it gives the impression of mountain peaks, to accord with the airline's name.

(Insignia — Plate 2)

117. Ransome's Nord Aviation N.262A N26210 in flight in early 1978.
(Photograph courtesy of Ransome Airlines)

118. Rich International's Curtiss C-46F N5370N in September 1977.
(Photograph from author's private collection)

119. Rio's de Havilland Canada DHC-6 Twin Otters N63RA, N19RA and N20RA at Dallas on 27 May 1978. (Photograph by W.C. Wann, Jr.)

120. Rocky Mountain's de Havilland Canada DHC-7 N27RM at Denver on 11 September 1978. (Photograph by W.C. Wann, Jr.)

121. ST. ANDREWS AIRWAYS

St. Andrews Airways, with its head office in Winnipeg, Manitoba, was formed in 1970, initially to operate cargo services with a Beech 18, and today flies passenger and cargo charter services from bases at Winnipeg, Island Lake and Selkirk (all in Manitoba).

Currently, St. Andrews has 2 Saunders ST-27s, a Twin Otter, a Beaver, 2 PA-23 Aztecs, a PA-22 Tri-Pacer, a Beech 3N and 4 Cessna 185s; a total of 12 aircraft.

The livery, as illustrated on ST-27 CF-LOL, consists of an all-white fuselage with a broad green cheatline, red titles and a stylised "A" on the tail-fin. The other ST-27, C-FJFH, wears a more ambitious scheme, with multi-cheatlines in red and a red fin; but this is not a true St. Andrews livery: it is the colours worn by the aircraft when operating for Aero Trades Western.

122. SAN JUAN AIRLINES

San Juan Airlines of Friday Harbor, Washington, offers scheduled commuter services to link Friday Harbor with Bellingham and Seattle/Tacoma (all in Washington state). Less regular services reach also the towns of Blakely, Crane, Lopez, Roche Harbor, Shaw, Stuart and Waldron.

San Juan's current fleet consists of 2 aircraft: a Cessna 207 (N1693U) and a Norseman (N27782)

The Norseman operates in an all-silver scheme, on which the only relief is the aircraft registration, in large black characters, and the small airline titling enclosed within a form of scroll (as illustrated, on the Cessna 207). The Cessna is more colourful, with an all-white fuselage, a light-red cheatline and dark-red trim. Note also the red cargo pannier beneath the fuselage.

(Insignia — Plate 4)

123. SCENIC AIRLINES

Scenic Airlines of Las Vegas, California, was formed in 1967 and operates scheduled commuter services to link Las Vegas with Grand Canyon, Yuma, Phoenix and Page (the last, seasonal) in Arizona; and Long Beach, Palm Springs, Carisbad and El Centro in California. The airline is perhaps more celebrated, however, for its truly "scenic" tours of the Grand Canyon (for which it has been awarded a Presidential citation for excellence in tourism), and for its pleasure flights around the famous Las Vegas Strip — usually two per afternoon — using the ageless Ford Tri-Motors.

Scenic's current fleet numbers 18 aircraft: 2 Ford Tri-Motors, 5 Metroliners, 6 Cessna 402s, 3 American-Jet Turbostar 402s, an American-Jet Turbostar 414 and a Twin Otter.

The Ford Tri-Motors, as illustrated, wear still the original paint-colour — Scenic holds now the last and final can of that original Ford pigmentation — and the airline has added a bright and cheerful "rainbow". The other aircraft have all-white fuselage and fins, with cheatlines in red and black; and these colours are repeated on the wing-tanks of the 402s. The stylised airline titling is worn generally on the tail-fin (at a slant to match the leading-edge); and the Metroliners carry also a smaller version of the titles on the for'ard fuselage, beneath the cheatlines.

(Insignia — Plate 2)

124. SEABOARD WORLD AIRLINES

Seaboard World Airlines of New York was formed in September 1946 as Seaboard and Western Airlines; and began operations — as a charter cargo airline — in May 1947. The company was awarded a scheduled freight licence in June 1955, and flew its first properly scheduled operation on 10 April 1956, from New York to Frankfurt. The name was changed in 1961 to Seaboard World Airlines, and permanent certification was granted in February 1966. Today, Seaboard World is one of the foremost air-freight carriers across the Atlantic, connecting several major US cities with Eire, the UK, Belgium, Holland, West Germany, France, Italy, Switzerland and the Scandinavian countries. Military charter work is also undertaken for the US Forces.

Currently, Seaboard World has 2 B.747Fs (with a third on order) and 11 DC-8Fs; a total of 13 aircraft. Two DC-10s are due to join the fleet shortly.

The B.747 livery, as illustrated, is a smart combination of gold, white, black and silver, with the "SW" logo standing out boldly in white on the gold tail-fin. Note that the DC-8s, while using the same colour combination, are in a slightly different scheme; having a white fuselage roof, a gold fin, black and gold cheatlines and a silver underside. Also, the DC-8s do not use the word "Containership".

(Insignia — Plate 4)

121.   St. Andrews' Saunders ST-27 CF-LOL in January 1978.

(Photograph from author's private collection)

122. San Juan's Cessna 207 Skywagon N1693U at Bellingham in August 1978.

(Photograph by John Kimberley)

123. Scenic's Ford 5-AT-C Tri-Motor N414H at Las Vegas on 18 May 1978.(Photograph by the author)

124. Seaboard World's Boeing 747-245F N701SW at London Heathrow in August 1974.

(Photograph by APN)

125. SIERRA PACIFIC AIRLINES

Sierra Pacific Airlines, with its headquarters at North Hollywood, California, was known originally as Trans Sierra Airlines; and first operated scheduled services in 1965. Following a re-organisation in 1973, the airline offers now scheduled passenger services which link Los Angeles (West Imperial Terminal) and Fresno with the Mammoth Lakes area of the Sierra Nevada and with Bishop (all in California) and Reno in Nevada. Charter services are also undertaken; and an extension of passenger services into San Francisco, Lake Tahoe and Orange County is proposed.

Sierra Pacific's current fleet numbers 4 aircraft: 3 Jetstreams and a CV.580.

The Jetstream livery, as illustrated, consists of an all-white fuselage, highlighted by orange and red cheatlines and by the attractive and unusual company motif — also in orange and red — on the fin. The CV.580 scheme, while essentially the same, has cheatlines of equal thickness (on the Jetstream, the orange cheat is much narrower than the red) and these go "straight-through", and not up the fin's trailing-edge. Also, the under-fuselage of the 580, beneath the cheatlines, is in a natural-metal finish.

(Insignia — Plate 3)

126. SLATE FALLS AIRWAYS

Slate Falls Airways of Souix Lookout, Ontario, was formed in 1958, and operates bush services throughout Ontario; providing in the main, transportation for hunters and fishermen into outpost locations such as Eagle Lake and Sachigo Lake. Charter services and aircraft overhaul facilities are also offered.

The airline has currently a fleet of 24 aircraft: a DC-3, a Twin Otter, a Beaver, an Otter, 5 Beech 18s, a PA-23 Aztec, a Piper J3C65, a Piper PA-12, a Beech Queen Air, a Beech Twin Bonanza, 2 Norseman, 2 Cessna 206s, a Cessna 185 and 5 Cessna 180s.

The livery, as illustrated, consists of a white upper fuselage and bare-metal underside, with a blue cheatline which goes "straight-through" and a blue trimline above, which turns up into a broad stripe across the fin. This stripe is broken to accommodate the "sfa" logo (note the lower case letters). Airline titling is in an attractive red script and carries beneath it the words "Souix Lookout, Ontario". Note also the repetition of fuselage colours on the engine cowlings.

127. SMB STAGE LINES

SMB Stage Lines (Sedalia-Marshall-Booneville Stage Lines) of Des Moines, Iowa, was formed in 1930 as a surface carrier and began its air operations in September 1967. The airline expanded to become a major passenger and cargo charter line, offering in addition daily commuter flights within its home state. In 1976, however, following a change in policy, SMB dropped its passenger operations and is now an all-cargo airline, flying to anywhere within the continental United States, and to Canada. True to its stagecoach connections, of course, SMB continues to carry the US mail, and retains also its bus and trucking operations.

In February 1978, SMB purchased 15 CV.600s from Texas International; but still operates in addition 7 DC-3s, 20 Beech 18s, a Beech C-45H, 2 Beech 99s, a PA-31 Navajo and 4 Volpar Westwinds — a total of 50 aircraft.

The livery, as illustrated, consists of a white upper fuselage and light-blue underside, with a dark-blue cheatline and airline titling, and a dark-blue "stagecoach" logo on the fin. Currently, the CV.600s are in basic Texas International livery (qv), but with the stagecoach symbol on the fin, replacing the Texas star, and SMB titles in the "gap" where Texas International titling was worn before.

(Insignia — Plate 4)

128. SOUTHERN AIR TRANSPORT

Southern Air Transport of Miami, Florida, was formed in July 1947 and undertook non-scheduled freight-work and Government contracts until becoming a supplemental carrier in January 1956. In the 1960s and early 1970s, the airline operated mainly in south-east Asia, generally under contract to the US Government; but surrendered its supplemental status in 1975, to become a Part 121 carrier (ie, an operator of large aircraft authorised to move private goods). Currently, however, Southern Air is seeking to regain supplemental authority, to work as such within USA and to Canada, Mexico, the Caribbean and Central and South America.

Southern Air has 2 aircraft: both Lockheed L.100 Hercules.

The livery, as illustrated, is extremely simple; consisting of a white upper fuselage and light-grey underside, with regular black, block-lettered airline titling and no form of logo or motif, other than the US flag on the tail. Note, however, that while Hercules N7984S (illustrated) has a very thin cheatline between the white and grey on the fuselage, and a black nose, the other Hercules (N9266R) has no cheat or trimline. but has a red nose.

125. Sierra Pacific's Handley Page HP.137 Jetstream N17RJ at Los Angeles (West Imperial) on 21 May 1978. (Photograph by the author)

126. Slate Falls' Douglas DC-3 C-FIAR at Winnipeg on 17 June 1978. (Photograph by F.H. Prior)

127. SMB Stage Lines' Douglas DC-3 N41447 in March 1976. (Photograph from APS files)

128. Southern Air Transport's Lockheed L.100-20 Hercules N7984S in July 1977.
(Photograph by John Kimberley)

129. SOUTHERN AIRWAYS

Southern Airways of Atlanta, Georgia, began scheduled services on 10 June 1949, with DC-3s, between Memphis (Tennessee) and Atlanta; and has since expanded to serve almost 70 US cities in 13 states, plus the District of Columbia. In addition, the airline has an international route, between Miami and Grand Cayman in the Cayman Islands; and it was over this route that Southern's first scheduled DC-9 service was inaugurated in December 1974. The airline undertakes also international passenger charters to Canada and the Bahamas, and domestic charters within the United States. At the time of writing, a merger is mooted with North Central Airlines (qv); but no final decisions have been taken.

Southern's current fleet comprises 27 DC-9s and 4 Metroliners; a total of 31 aircraft.

The livery consists of an all-white fuselage (but for a bare-metal understrip), with a broad, bold cheatline in dark-blue. The cheatline is set unusually high, to leave only a white strip along the roof of the fuselage, and sweeps up to embrace most of the tail-fin. Airline titling is in white, as is the stylised "S", in triple bands, on the fin. Note also that fleet numbers are carried both on the nosewheel doors and on the for'ard fin.

(Insignia — Plate 2)

130. SOUTHWEST AIRLINES

Southwest Airlines of Dallas, Texas, was formed as Air Southwest on 15 March 1967, and became almost immediately involved in a series of legal battles, in which other carriers attempted to prevent the airline's operating; but in March 1971, the company changed its name to Southwest Airlines, and began operations on 18 June 1971. The airline has flourished; and today provides all-jet intra-state commuter services, linking Dallas, Houston, Harlingen, San Antonio, Corpus Christi, Lubbock, Midland/Odessa, El Paso and Austin. The current fleet consists of 10 B.737-200s, with 6 more on order.

The airline's "heart" or "love" symbol (not worn on the aircraft) stems from the fact that Southwest operates from Love Field, Dallas; something which was a major factor in the airline's legal tussles: Love Field is Dallas' "downtown" airport, and competitors wanted Southwest moved to the then-new but less-convenient Dallas-Fort Worth Regional Airport.

The livery — said to be orange, red and desert gold — is bright, original and eye-catching. Note that formerly, the titling read "Southwest Airlines" (with one word on the after fuselage and the other going up the fin); but now, only the "Southwest" is used, as illustrated. Note also the small black anti-dazzle panel on the nose.

(Insignia — Plate 2)

131. STOL AIR COMMUTER

Stol Air Commuter (Stol Air Inc) of San Rafael, California, was formed in 1972, and offers high-frequency intra-state commuter services, to link San Francisco International Airport with Concord, Napa, Oakland, San Rafael and Santa Rosa.

Stol Air operates with an all-Britten-Norman fleet, having 4 Islanders and a Trislander; and has the distinction of being the first US carrier to put its livery on a Trislander, having taken delivery of the aircraft at the end of 1977.

The Trislander livery, as illustrated, consists of an all-white fuselage, with light-and dark-blue cheatlines which turn up through the after part of the tail-fin; the company logo is worn on the lower fin, and is repeated in the "O" of the airline titles, carried on the tail-engine. The Islanders are essentially in the same scheme, although their titles are slanted up the leading-edge of the fin, and topped by the company logo; except for N63JA, which wears a conventional "straight-through" cheatline in yellow, with a matching horizontal band across the fin. Titling and logo remain, however, as for the other Islanders.

(Insignia — Plate 4)

132. SUMMIT AIRLINES

Summit Airlines of Philadelphia, Pennsylvania, was formed in 1966 as the Delaware Air Freight Co., to operate freight services between Millville, New Jersey and Philadelphia. While Delaware Air Freight expanded, however, the name contracted in common usage: to Del-Air. This led to possible confusion with Delta Air Lines, particularly as Del-Air's route network had extended well beyond its origins in the Delaware Valley; and in 1974, following discussions between the two companies, Del-Air changed its name to Summit Airlines. Today, Summit operates scheduled all-cargo services in 12 eastern states, serving some 19 cities which included New York, Boston, Buffalo, Atlanta, Birmingham and Washington DC. In addition, the airline undertakes cargo charter work.

Currently, Summit has 13 aircraft: 3 DC-3s, 3 CV.580s and 7 Skyvans.

The livery consists of a double-cheatline in green and blue, on an overall white fuselage, with a stylised "SA" motif on the tail-fins, and green/blue/green stripes beneath. Note also, the unusual form of airline titling; with "Summit" in solid green lettering and "Airlines" in an outlined style in blue — which may be only faintly discernible in the photograph.

(Insignia — Plate 4)

129.   Southern's McDonnell Douglas DC-9-14 N3306L in August 1973.   (Photograph from APS files)

130.   Southwest's Boeing 737-2A1 N25SW in November 1977.

(Photograph from author's private collection)

131. Stol Air's Britten-Norman BN-2A Mk.III Trislander N403JA at San Francisco on 25 May 1978.
(Photograph by the author)

132. Summit's Short SC-7 Skyvan 3 N70DA in March 1976.   (Photograph from APS files)

133. SWIFT AIRE LINES

Swift Aire Lines began life in March 1969 with one Piper Navajo and the idea of offering professional air services to the smaller communities in California, and has been expanding rapidly ever since. Ideally placed with a home-base at San Luis Obispo (almost equidistant between San Francisco and Los Angeles), Swift Aire now serves additionally Santa Maria, Los Angeles, Bakersfield, Visalia, Fresno, Paso Robles, San Jose, San Francisco and Sacramento; and has routes-pending to Redding and Santa Barbara. Charter work is also undertaken.

The current fleet consists of 10 aircraft: 6 Riley Herons and 4 Nord 262s.

The airline's original livery evolved from the simple fact that the Piper Navajos were delivered in a stock blue-on-white colour scheme, to which the airline's founder and president, Mr. Charles G. Wiswell, added a red logo to personalise his aircraft. In 1977, however, Swift Aire introduced an entirely new livery, common to both Herons and N.262s, consisting of an all-white fuselage, with a tripe-cheatline in light-blue, light-green and dark-green moving up into the tail-fin, where the light-blue and light-green serve as a background for the dark-green stylised "SA" logo. Airline titling appears for'ard, with a word on either side of the cheatlines; and note also, just aft of the small break in the cheats (adjacent to the titles), the original Swift Aire motif — an up-pointed wing — in dark-green, coming up out of the dark-green cheat.

(Insignia — Plate 1)

134. TEXAS INTERNATIONAL AIRLINES

Texas International Airlines of Houston, Texas, was formed in 1940 as Aviation Enterprises, changed its name to Trans-Texas Airways in July 1947, and began scheduled services in October of the same year. The airline took its current name in 1968; and today, serves all major points in Texas, and terminals in the states of New Mexico, Nevada, California, Utah, Colorado, Arkansas, Louisiana, Tennessee and Mississippi; with international services across the Mexican border to Mexico City and Monterrey. In addition, route-extensions into Arizona and several other Mexican terminals are proposed.

Having disposed of most of its CV.600s to SMB Stage Lines (qv), the airline has now only 3 of the type; but has 26 DC-9s, with more on order. It is of note that the DC-9-14 illustrated here, N1301T, was the Douglas prototype (as N9DC) and is to be retired shortly to a museum, for preservation as the first-ever DC-9.

Highlight of the livery is the stylised five-point star — of Texas, the Lone Star State — on the fin. The fuselage is all-white (but for a bare-metal understrip); the lower cheatline is in red, and continuous; while the upper cheat, in blue, is broken to house airline titling and the US flag, before sweeping up into the fin. Note, however, that the leading and upper edges of the fin are in white, in direct continuation from the fuselage roof.

(Insignia — Plate 3)

135. TIME AIR

Time Air of Lethbridge, Alberta, was known originally as Lethbridge Air Services, and took its current title in 1969. Today, the airline operates scheduled passenger services within Alberta, linking Lethbridge with Calgary, Medicine Hat, Red Deer, Edmonton and Grand Prairie; and holds additionally permits for domestic and international charters.

Currently, Time Air has 5 aircraft: 2 Twin Otters and 3 Shorts 330s.

The Shorts 330 livery, as illustrated, consists of an all-white fuselage, with two broad cheatlines; the upper in red, and the lower in greenish-brown. The greenish-brown colour leads the company logo on the tail-fins, with the red colour aft of it, to form a wide stripe. Note that this stripe appears both on outboard and inboard sides of the fins. The Twin Otter livery is essentially the same, except that a triple-cheatline (in greenish-brown/red/greenish-brown) is used, and airline titles appear beneath the cheat; and where the Shorts 330 engines are in bare-metal, the Twin Otters are painted black and white.

(Insignia — Plate 1)

136. TRADEWINDS AVIATION

Tradewinds Aviation, based at Vancouver Airport South, British Columbia, is a relative newcomer to B.C. coastal operations, for which it qualified by the acquisition of Harrison Airways' light-seaplane licences. Today, the airline operates charter, air ambulance and contract flying services from Vancouver; and additionally offers aircraft maintenance.

The current fleet consists of an Islander, 2 PA-31 Navajos, a PA-23 Aztec, a Cessna 310, a Cessna 206 and a Cessna 185.

Although the livery differs in detail between types of aircraft, it consists essentially of an all-white fuselage with cheatlines (or a cheatline and trim) in tan and dark-brown. All aircraft carry airline titling in the form illustrated on the Islander (ie, with "Tradewinds" in block lettering, and "Aviation" in script form); and most, but not all, wear the "white bird" logo, either on the nose or the fin.

133. Swift Aire's Nord Aviation N.262A N418SA at San Francisco on 25 May 1978.
(Photograph by the author)

134. Texas International's McDonnell Douglas DC-9-14 N1301T "Denver" at Kansas City in July 1978.
(Photograph by J.H. Williamson)

135. Time Air's Shorts 330 C-GTAM in August 1977. (Photograph by John Kimberley)

136. Tradewinds' Britten-Norman BN-2A Islander C-GIPF in August 1978.

(Photograph by John Kimberley)

137. TRANSAIR

Transair of Winnipeg, Manitoba, was formed on 8 April 1947 as Central Northern Airways; and took its current title in 1956, when CNA merged with the Churchill-based operator Arctic Wings. In November 1969, Transair took over Midwest Airlines, which continues as a separate division with an all-helicopter fleet. Today, Transair operates extensive scheduled services over a wide network serving Manitoba, Ontario, the Northwest Territories and the Yukon. Charter services are also undertaken, throughout North America and to the Caribbean and Mexico; as are DEWline resupply flights.

Currently, Transair has 7 aircraft: 3 B.737-200s, 2 F.28s and 2 YS-11As.

The livery consists of a yellow upper fuselage and bare-metal underside, separated by a white-trimmed, brown cheatline which turns up through the trailing-edge of the tail-fin. Airline titling is in black, in an attractive lower-case form, and most aircraft carry names: YS-11A C-FTAK is "Norway House", for example; and F-28 C-FTAY is "Fort Prince of Wales". Note also that on the F.28s, the upper half of the engines are in brown, and carry there the Canadian flag.

(Insignia — Plate 2)

138. TRANS CATALINA AIRLINES

Trans Catalina Airlines, based at Long Beach Airport, California, is a new operator, having commenced services on 8 February 1978. The airline, a subsidiary of National Jet Industries of Orange County, flies regular scheduled services between Long Beach and the Pebbly Beach Terminal at Avalon, Santa Catalina Island; thus rivalling Catalina Airlines (qv).

Trans Catalina's fleet consists of 3 Mallards: N36DF, named "Spirit of Avalon", N95DF ("Catalina Clipper") and N51151 ("Island Princess").

The livery is a bright combination of white, brown and orange; with a white fuselage, tail-fin and wings, and orange and brown cheatlines, engines and floats. The aircraft's name is worn in small scripted letters at the point of the innermost cheatline; and Trans Catalina titles are carried above the cheatlines aft, and on the inboard side of the floats. Note also that while the company logo is worn boldly on the fin, the aircraft registration is in tiny characters, at the very stern of the hull, beneath the cheats.

(Insignia — Plate 3)

139. TRANS INTERNATIONAL AIRLINES

Trans International Airlines of Oakland, California, was formed in 1948 as Los Angeles Air Service, and adopted its current title in 1960. In 1962, the airline became a wholly-owned subsidiary of the Studebaker Corporation, but reverted to independent ownership in 1964. In 1968, ownership was sold to the Transamerica Corporation (who own also, inter alia, United Artists Pictures and Budge Rent-A-Car). A merger in December 1976 with Saturn Airways brought TIA not only 12 Hercules aircraft, but further expertise in the cargo field: all TIA's jets are convertible from passenger to cargo roles. As a charter and supplemental carrier, TIA operates throughout USA and to Europe, Africa, the Caribbean, Asia, the South Pacific, the Far East and Central and South America.

Currently, TIA has 3 DC-10-30s, 11 DC-8CFs, 11 Hercules and 9 Electras; a total of 34 aircraft.

The current livery was introduced in April 1976, to link the airline more closely with its parent company. Highlight of the design is the large letter "T" on the tail-fin. This is, in fact,a decal; a pressure-sensitive film developed by the 3M company and much more rapid in application than normal painting. The decal was designed and prepared by Graphic Marking Systems of Los Angeles; and the overall design was created by Soyster and Ohrenschall Inc. of San Francisco. Note also that the green and blue fin-top stripes are repeated on the outer wings.

(Insignia — Plate 1)

140. TRANS NORTH TURBO AIR

Trans North Turbo Air of Whitehorse, Yukon, was incorporated as a limited company in June 1966, and began operations in February of the following year. Today, the company offers charter air services throughout northwestern Canada, using an integrated fleet of fixed-wing aircraft and helicopters.

Currently, this fleet numbers 28 aircraft: a Twin Otter, a Cessna Titan, a Cessna 402B, a PA-34 Seneca, an Otter, 2 Turbo Beavers, a Beaver, 2 Beech 95 Barons, a Cessna 185, 6 Bell 47Gs, 9 JetRangers, an Alouette and an S-55B/T

Trans North's aircraft appear in a variety of colour schemes (often, as delivered). For instance, the two twin-prop Cessnas are in quite different schemes: the Cessna 402 is, as illustrated, in basically a white and orange scheme; while the Titan is in white and blue. Standard to most aircraft, however, is the simple black block-lettered airline titling; and note that this says merely "Trans North", and not the full company title.

(Insignia — Plate 4)

137. Transair's Boeing 737-2A9C C-FTAN "Fort William" at Toronto on 4 August 1978.
(Photograph by Russell Brown)

138. Trans Catalina's Grumman G.73 Mallard N95DF "Catalina Clipper" at Pebbly Beach on 20 May 1978.
(Photograph by the author)

139. Trans International's McDonnell Douglas DC-8-63CF N4869T at London Heathrow in February 1978. (Photograph by A.J. Kemsley)

140. Trans North's Cessna 402B C-GWLE in April 1977. (Photograph by John Kimberley)

141. TRANS-PROVINCIAL AIRLINES

Trans-Provincial Airlines of Terrace, British Columbia, was formed in 1960; and offers extensive scheduled passenger services in British Columbia; with an international route from Prince Rupert to Ketchikan in Alaska. The airline has bases at Terrace, Prince Rupert, Sandspit and Ocean Falls, from the last of which it undertakes charter work, in addition.

Trans-Provincial has currently 19 aircraft: 3 Otters, a Beech 18, 5 Goose amphibians, 8 Beavers, a Cessna 185 and a Cessna 180.

The livery, as illustrated, consists of an all-yellow fuselage, with a dark-blue cheatline, wing-tips and company logo, on the fin. Normally, small airline titles — in the form "Trans-Provincial" — are carried in block letters above the cheatline and just aft of the passenger-door; but at the time when our photograph was taken, the aircraft therein was on lease to Gulf-Air Aviation (qv). Note, also, the black antidazzle panel on the nose.

(Insignia — Plate 4)

142. TRANS WORLD AIRLINES

Trans World Airlines has its origins in the same Western Air Express that was the forerunner of Western Airlines (qv). A merger in 1930 of Western Air Express and Transcontinental Air Transport brought forth Transcontinental and Western Air (TWA); but the merger was short-lived and the WAE element was bought out (to become Western Airlines), while TWA went on to flourish equally, and to change its name in 1950 to Trans World Airlines. TWA is now one of the largest airlines in the world, with comprehensive routes within USA and to Europe and the Middle East. The executive offices are in New York City, with the training centre and aircraft overhaul base at Kansas City, Missouri.

Currently, TWA has 186 aircraft: 11 B.747-100s, 96 B.707s, 26 L.1011s, 39 B.727-200s (with 14 more on order), 35 B.727-100Cs and 14 DC-9-15s.

Although traditionalists felt a pang at the passing of TWA's "twin globe" logo and old "red dart" scheme, the current livery manages to be both reminiscent of the old and yet contemporary. Designed by TWA's Director of Corporate Design, Mr. Jules Rondepierre, it retains the "dart" shape in the double-cheatline, but offers more modern imagery in the logo and titles. The livery was worn first by B.747 N53111, rolled out at Kansas City on 30 November 1974; and is illustrated here on L.1011 N31030, which inaugurated "Tristar" services to London Heathrow on 1 May 1978 (see legend on aircraft's nose).

(Insignia — Plate 4)

143. UNITED AIRLINES

United Airlines of Chicago, Illinois, was formed on 1 July 1931 as the management company for Boeing Air Transport, National Air Transport, Pacific Air Transport and Varney Air Lines. (Varney was bought out of the company again in 1934, and later became Continental Airlines (qv).). United went on to take over Capital Airlines in June 1961, in what was at the time the biggest-ever airline merger. Today, United is one of the largest airlines in the world, and probably the world's biggest privately-owned airline in terms of passenger-miles flown and passengers carried. The company serves the USA from the Atlantic seaboard to the Pacific coast and beyond to Hawaii, and from Mexico to Vancouver in Canada.

United's enormous fleet numbers current 361 all-jet aircraft: 18 B.747-100s, 37 DC-10-10s, 98 DC-8s, 34 B.727-200s (plus 40 more on order), 115 B.727-100s and 59 B.737-200s.

The current livery was introduced on 17 June 1974, on DC-8 N8031U, and the "double U" motif was the first entirely new symbol to be introduced by United since the former "shield" motif went into service in 1936. The livery, designed by Saul Bass and Associates of Los Angeles, incorporated also a titling change from United Air Lines to United Airlines. Note that the fuselage is genuinely all-white, and does not have a metal understripe as favoured by many airlines.

(Insignia — Plate 4)

144. WARDAIR CANADA

Wardair (Wardair Canada (1975) Ltd) of Edmonton, Alberta, has origins in the Polaris Charter Co, formed in 1946 by Maxwell W. Ward (Wardair's current president) to fly bush operations from Yellowknife. Wardair was formed in 1953 to continue these operations; and became Wardair Canada Ltd. in 1962, when operating authority was altered to embrace international charters. The airline went public on 18 September 1967 (Mr Ward remains a majority shareholder) and took the title Wardair Canada (1975) Ltd. on 1 January 1976. Today, the company offers international charters to worldwide destinations; but maintains its services throughout the Canadian Arctic with a local division still based at Yellowknife.

Currently, Wardair has 12 aircraft: 2 B.747-100s, 2 B.707s, a Dash 7, a Bristol 170 Freighter, 5 Twin Otters and an MU-2B; 2 B.747-200s, 2 DC-10-30s and another Dash 7 are on order.

The standard livery, as illustrated, has a white upper fuselage and bare-metal underside; with a "straight-through" cheatline in dark-blue, and a red cheatline which starts aft of the airline titles and sweeps back and up through the fin, on which it breaks to accommodate the company logo. Note, however, that the Arctic division aircraft do not wear the standard scheme; eg, the Dash 7 has a dark-blue fuselage top, underside and fin upper and leading edges, and a wide white cheatline embellished by red trimlines which widen as they run aft, to give a red fin and rear fuselage.

(Insignia — Plate 4)

141. Trans-Provincial's de Havilland Canada DHC-2 Beaver C-FJBP in August 1978.
(Photograph by John Kimberley)

142.   TWA's Lockheed L.1011-193B N31030 at London Heathrow in May 1978.
(Photograph by A.J. Kemsley)

143. United's McDonnell Douglas DC-10-10 N1804U "Curtis Barkes" at San Francisco on 25 May 1978.
(Photograph by the author)

144. Wardair's Boeing 747-124 C-FFUN "Romeo Vachon" departing London Gatwick in May 1977.
(Photograph by the author)

145. WEST COAST AIR SERVICES

West Coast Air Services, based at Vancouver International Airport, British Columbia, was formed in 1931 as Gilbert's Flying Service; and today, operates extensive charter services from bases at Vancouver, Nanaimo and Nelson, all in British Columbia. Scheduled services are flown also, under contract to Pacific Western, to serve Ocean Falls, Bella Bella, Bella Coola, Namu, Tahsis and Tofino, from Vancouver.

West Coast Air's current fleet consists of 25 aircraft: 5 Mallards, a Turbo Mallard, a Cessna 402A, 5 Beavers, an Otter, a Cessna T210L, 6 Cessna 185s, a Cessna 182 and 4 Cessna 180s.

The airline uses a number of livery variations. Most aircraft are in the standard livery (as illustrated) of a white fuselage, with blue cheatline and blue "bird" motif on the fin; and these include Mallards C-FHUB, C-GENT and C-GIRL; Twin Otters C-GKNR and C-FPAE; and Navajo C-GPOW. Beavers C-FAXI and C-FOSP are, however, among another set of aircraft which wear the same livery except that cheatlines and logo are in red instead of blue. The small Cessnas, such as Cessna 185 C-GIFJ, are also in a red and white livery, but generally do not carry the logo at all. Turbo Mallard C-GHUM does not carry the logo, either; and is in an odd scheme with a blue and white striped tail, a broad blue cheatline with a thinner gold cheatline and a red trimline beneath. Most colourful of all is Otter C-FUJM, which has no logo, but a bright orange tail, a mustard-coloured fuselage and double-cheatlines in slate-grey.

(Insignia — Plate 4)

146 WESTERN AIRLINES

Western Airlines, known until 1941 as Western Air Express, is the sole survivor of a number of fledgling airlines which got their start when the US Post Office granted air mail contracts to private companies in 1925. In fact, Western's first flight was on 17 April 1926, using a Douglas M-2 open-cockpit biplane. Today, the airline is based in Los Angeles, with routes that extend northwards to Seattle and on to Alaska, eastwards to Minneapolis/St. Paul in Minnesota, and westwards to the Hawaiian islands. International segments reach Vancouver, Calgary and Edmonton in Canada, and Acapulco and Mexico City in Mexico. The airline can claim also a "transcontinental" designation, with a nonstop service between Los Angeles and Miami, using DC-10s — which Western calls "Spaceships".

Currently, Western has 9 DC-10-10s, 5 B.707s, 14 B.720s, 32 B.727-200s and 25 B.737-200s; a total of 85 aircraft.

The current livery was introduced in 1970, replacing the venerable "Indian head" scheme, and was designed by Lippincott and Margulies Inc, of New York. It consists of an all-white fuselage (but for a bare-metal understrip) with a broad red cheatline which incorporates the company logo at the for'ard end. Airline titling is attractive and bold, in black and white, and appears both on the fuselage and the tail-fin.

(Insignia — Plate 2)

147. WIEN AIR ALASKA

Wien Air Alaska enjoys the claim of being the state's oldest airline, and of serving more of Alaska than any other carrier — currently over 170 communities in Alaska and the Yukon — from its base in Anchorage. One of the few remaining major airlines to retain its founder's name — that of Noel Wien, an aviation pioneer of the twenties and thirties — Wien Air Alaska can trace its history back through Wien Consolidated Airlines (until 1973), Wien Alaska Airlines (until 1968) and the Wien Brothers Airline (established in 1927). Figuring prominently in Alaskan aviation, too, is the company's current chairman, Mr Ray Petersen, who ran his own airline until a merger (with Wien) in 1968.

Wien Air's current fleet numbers 22 aircraft: 7 B.737-200s, 4 FH-227s, 4 F-27s, 4 Twin Otters, 2 Skyvans and a Mallard.

The airline shares its colours — blue and gold — with the state of Alaska, and the logo was designed by Stimson Advertising of Seattle, Washington. Note the thin gold trimline beneath the white of the fuselage; and the fact that in the airline titling, the "Wien" is in small scripted form, against the bolder, block-lettered "Air Alaska".

(Insignia — Plate 4)

148. WILDERNESS AIRLINE

The Wilderness Airline (Wilderness Airline 1975 Ltd) of Williams Lake, British Columbia, provides both charter and scheduled intra-province services from bases at Williams Lake, Bella Coola and Nimpo Lake; and other terminals linked thereby are South Bentinck, Kimsquit, Puntzi, Tatla, One Eye, Charlotte and Anahim. Flying training is also undertaken, at Bella Coola.

Currently, Wilderness has 5 aircraft: 3 Beavers, an Islander and a Cessna 185.

The livery consists of a yellow fuselage, divided by a broad white cheatline which develops as it runs aft, to embrace half of the tail-fin. The black anti-dazzle panel on the nose is extended to fill the for'ard fuselage section above the cheatline; and airline titling is designed cleverly to impart a "backwoods" flavour, in black-edged yellow. A "Beaver" legend is carried on the crew door, with the aircraft name aft of it, on the passenger door.

(Insignia — Plate 4)

145. West Coast Air's Grumman G.73 Mallard C-FHUB in August 1978.(Photograph by John Kimberley)

146. Western's McDonnell Douglas DC-10-10 N902WA in May 1975.

(Photograph from author's private collection)

147. Wien Air Alaska's Fairchild F-27A N2709R on 3 October 1977.   (Photograph by Ben Knowles, Jr.)

148.   Wilderness Airline's de Havilland Canada DHC-2 Beaver C-FJPL "Bella Coola" at Vancouver in January 1977.   (Photograph by Phil Hanson)

149. WORLD AIRWAYS

World Airways of Oakland, California, was formed in 1948 as a charter operator, and has since expanded to become one of the world's leading non-scheduled airlines; a fact due in no small part to its current president, Edward J. Daly, who rescued the company and its debts in 1950. The airline has authority to conduct passenger operations within the United States, and to almost all overseas destinations; and a slightly more-restrictive authority is held in respect of cargo charters.

Currently, World has 3 B.747-200s (2 leased out), 2 DC-10-30s, 5 DC-8-63s, a B.707 (leased out), 3 B.727-100s (all leased out) and a CV.340; a total of 15 aircraft. A B.747F and 4 DC-10-30Fs are on order.

The current livery was first seen in December 1977, when the first of World's DC-10s (N103WA) was rolled out by McDonnell Douglas. It consists of a white upper fuselage and bare-metal underside, divided by a broad red, gold-trimmed cheatline. This develops as it runs aft, to leave the lower fin in a gold/red/gold/red arrangement; and the fin carried also the company logo and the US flag. The "globe" symbol appears again in the cheatline for'ard, and airline titling is in red, slightly-slanted block letters.

(Insignia – Plate 1)

150. WORLDWAYS AIRLINES

Worldways Airlines of East Mississauga, Ontario, was formed in 1976, and offers a variety of charter services. Canada Learjet Ltd. is an associated company of the airline, which – in fact – operates 2 Learjet 35s, as well as 2 CV.640s and an HS.125.

For some long time, Worldways has operated its aircraft without airline titles: CV.640 C-FPWT, for instance, has worn the standard livery with the Worldways logo on the fin, but no titling, since the airline's formation. With the introduction of the second CV.640 (C-FPWU) in mid-1978, however, titles were seen for the first time; and the full livery can now be taken to be as illustrated: a white upper fuselage and bare-metal underside, with a double-cheatline in two values of blue; and the Worldways logo and titles in the darker shade. Note that, not unnaturally, both World and Worldways use a "globe" symbol as the logo; but Worldways' versions is much enhanced by the attractive "broken" form of "W" worn thereon.

(Insignia – Plate 4)

151. WRIGHT AIRLINES

Wright Airlines of Cleveland, Ohio, began scheduled operations in 1966, with commuter services from Cleveland to Detroit (Michigan), Pittsburgh (Pennsylvania) and Dayton and Columbus in Ohio; and absorbed both Tyme Airlines of Columbus and Air Commuter Airlines of Cleveland in 1968. Today, the airline offers six round-trips daily between downtown Cleveland and downtown Detroit; plus two round-trips daily between Columbus and Cleveland, and Columbus and Detroit. In addition, Wright can offer a "Red Carpet Charter Service" to anywhere within the continental USA, Canada, Mexico or the Caribbean. An express air freight service is also available on normal routes. The current fleet consists of 6 CV.600s.

Although trading as Wright Airlines, the company is properly "Wright Air Lines Inc" and this is reflected in the airline titling on the aircraft — which wear a smart yellow, orange and red triple-cheatline on a white fuselage, with the company logo displayed boldly just for'ard of the cabin windows. Note, too, the black-anti-dazzle panel on the nose; and that the aircraft registration is worn unusually high on the fuselage, aft of the titling.

(Insignia — Plate 4)

152. ZANTOP INTERNATIONAL AIRLINES

Zantop International Airlines, with its headquarters at Detroit-Willow Run Airport, Ypsilanti, Michigan, was formed in May 1972 by the Zantop Brothers; and the Zantop family remain major stockholders. The airline carries out extensive cargo charter services and contract work.

The current fleet consists of 42 aircraft: 2 DC-8-33Fs, 12 DC-6s, 14 CV.640Fs and 14 Electras.

Although Zantop's aircraft have operated in a variety of liveries over the years, that illustrated can be taken to be standard: a white upper fuselage and bare-metal underside, with a broad cheatline, in red and repeated in a parallel strip on the white fin. Note that the cheatline narrows and curves at both extremities; and that the silver underside curves away, too, to leave an all-white nose. Airline titling is in red capital letters, and is set unusually centrally on the fuselage, directly above the wings.

(Insignia — Plate 4)

149. World's McDonnell Douglas DC-8-63CF N805WA in May 1978.

150. Worldways' Convair CV.640 C-FPWU on 4 August 1978.   (Photograph by Russell Brown)

151. Wright's Convair CV.600 N74850 in January 1978.   (Photograph from author's private collection)

152.   Zantop International's Lockheed L.188AF Electra N286F in July 1977.

(Photograph by John Kimberley)

AEROBEC LTEE 3

133

135

KENTING 77

Catalina Airlines 39

18

panarctic 108

2

A·A 23

98

65

N 96

PDA 114

95

GA 67

PAN AM 107

17

149

38

99

85

93

G 61

66

GNA

HARBOR AIR 69

139

ISLAND AIRLINES 75

PSA 105

FEDERAL EXPRESS 55

11

72

AIR SUNSHINE 15

MARTIN AIR 86

146

57

Athabaska AIRWAYS LTD. 27

Rio 119

CHALK'S INTERNATIONAL 40

112

97

BI 33

PEM·AIR LIMITED 110

68

M 84

63

137

120

BRADLEY Air Services 32

74

am 13

Island Air

CONTACT AIRWAYS LTD. 45

60

SCENIC AIRLINES, INC. 123

29

21

Aloha

AIRLINES 130

129

BAJA CORTEZ AIRLINES

SOUTHWEST

FLYING TIGERS

PTARMIGAN AIRWAYS LTD. 115

59

73

117

113

43 PRINAIR

FLYING FIREMAN 58

88

125

134

9

air florida

78

57

MIDSTATE 87

FIRSTAIR 32

50

42

49

51

PACIFIC ALASKA AIRLINES 103

92

53

138 TCA

6

MNA 91

71

101 OKANAGAN HELICOPTERS LTD.

102

48 CP Air

24

117

106

94

harrison air 70

B 31

34

22

46

19

AIR WEST 16

5